God,
are you
talking to
Me?

Dr. Rod D. Hoskins

GOD, ARE YOU TALKING TO ME? ©

By Dr. Rod D. Hoskins

ROD HOSKINS MINISTRIES, Inc.

P.O. BOX 3314

WESTERVILLE, OHIO 43086

Printed in the United States of America

ISBN 9780692833544

GOD, ARE YOU TALKING TO ME? Is dedicated to the Holy Spirit of God. His many words of encouragement, guidance, and patience have inspired me to write this book in an effort to train and encourage God's people to learn and discern the voice of God.

Thank You, Lord!

John 10:25-30

Jesus answered them, "I told you, and you do not believe. The works that I do in My Father's name, they bear witness of Me. 26 But you do not believe, because you are not of My sheep, as I said to you. 27 <u>My sheep hear My voice, and I know them, and they follow Me</u>. 28 And I give them eternal life, and they shall never perish; neither shall anyone snatch them out of My hand. 29 My Father, who has given them to Me, is greater than all; and no one is able to snatch them out of My Father's hand. 30 I and My Father are one."

FOREWORD

It is estimated that there are more than six billion people on this planet we call earth. It is believed that more than one billion of them are confessed Christians, or Followers of Christ. As you read this introduction, you may say that you are one of these believers. Most confessed Christians understand that their relationship to God is only available through faith in Jesus Christ. However, if I were to ask the vast majority of confessed believers today if they have ever heard the voice of God, most would reply that they have never heard the voice of the Holy Spirit. This creates an interesting dilemma and question to the Church. If there are so many confessed followers of Christ, how is it that so many do not hear the voice of God?

This question is extremely relevant, considering Jesus Himself said in John 10:27, *"My sheep hear My voice, and I know them, and they follow Me"*. Jesus also made this statement in John 18:37 when Pilate asked Him;

> *"Are You a king then?" Jesus answered, "You say rightly that I am a king. For this cause I was born, and for this cause I have come into the world, that I should bear witness to the truth. Everyone who is of the truth hears My voice."*

Not only should those who follow Jesus hear His voice, but also those who desire to follow should hear His voice. *"If anyone hears My voice and opens the door, I will come in to him and dine with him, and he with Me"* (Rev. 3:20). Therefore, the question to every confessed Christian is this: If you are not hearing the voice of God, why not? Could it be that you have not been taught how to hear or recognize God's voice?

It is the goal of this book to teach those who want to learn how to hear God's voice and to fulfill the *Great Commission* Jesus gave the Church:

> *"Go therefore and make disciples of all the nations, baptizing them in the name of the Father and of the Son and of the Holy Spirit, teaching them to observe all things that I have commanded you; and lo, I am with you always, even to the end of the age."* Amen. Matt. 28:19-20

As a side note, you will discover that I use many Hebrew and Greek definitions throughout this book. **Why do I reference the Hebrew and Greek?** Over the centuries, the English language has changed many of the definitions or meanings of its words. I find that the Hebrew and Greek definitions gives us a more complete meaning of words translated, if we explore them in their original Hebrew and Greek definitions.

An example of this is found with the English word 'comforter'. When used in the English language, it is most often defined as one called alongside to comfort...to show compassion in time of sorrow, or need. However, in the Greek, it takes a more active role as someone summoned to one's side to plead one's case before a judge in court; a counsel for the defense; a legal assistant; an advocate (Thayer's Greek Lexicon).

I have used my best effort not to confuse the reader, but to seek a more complete understanding of what the Holy Spirit's original conveyance is intended to accomplish through the Holy Scriptures.

TABLE OF CONTENTS

CHAPTER 1

EARS TO HEAR

One morning in the summer of 1978, I awoke to start the day in my usual pattern of prayer, and time reading the Bible. I found this to be the best time of day for me to concentrate on the scriptures without thinking about all the cares of the day. I left home for work and confronted the usual traffic congestion on Route 62 driving into downtown Columbus, Ohio. This morning however, would be different from any I had ever experienced before.

As I was driving, I heard someone speak to me in what I perceived was an audible male voice. He said, *I am going to put you in your own business.* My first response was to turn and see who was sitting in the backseat of my car. Upon finding no one in the backseat, I thought to myself: "Great! I must still be asleep, because now I am hearing voices from someone that is not there".

Having returned home that evening, I shared with my wife what I had experienced that morning on the trip to the office. Her response offered two possibilities for what had happened. First, had I just imagined hearing a voice? Or, secondly, maybe God was talking to me. Either way, with a new house, a new baby, and bills to pay, she was not very receptive to the idea of a career change. This prompted me to put the incident on the shelf for a while.

It was a few weeks later that she and I went to a special meeting at a local church to hear a guest speaker from Tulsa, Oklahoma. At the end of the service, he said he had a prophetic word from the Lord for two men in the audience. He pointed to me and another young man, and asked us to come forward and receive what God had to say.

He proceeded to tell me that God was calling me into a new business and that it would be something different from what I was currently doing. I had never received a prophetic word from the Lord like this before, so I was a little apprehensive as to what it meant.

It was a few months after this event that my wife and I were attending another meeting held by another traveling minister. As he was speaking, he pointed to our location and said, "God is calling someone in this section into their own business".

Needless to say, I was still a little skeptical, as I had heard stories of how people had received a so-called word from God telling them to go to Africa or some other remote parts of the world. Then to find out when they were there, that they had missed God and were not called as missionaries.

It was shortly after these events that God revealed to me a truth from Matthew 18:16, *"by the mouth of two or three witnesses every **word** may be established."* This passage of scripture, and the preceding events moved me to make decisions that would alter my life forever. It prompted me to study the Bible in ways I had not pursued previously.

After buying a Bible concordance and a Greek dictionary, I proceeded to study just what this passage meant. Was God really talking to me?

I had several questions that needed answers and I needed God to reveal these answers to me:

1. God, do you still talk to your people today?

2. How do we know when You are talking to us? Are we to look for a burning bush?

3. Is it okay to ask for a sign from God?

4. Is it only through Your Bible that You talk to us?

5. Do you still have prophets today, and are we to be led in life by prophets?

6. God, if You still talk to us today, how do we know it is You talking to us and not our own imagination or something else?

7. God, who am I that You would talk to me?

These questions brought me to the last and most important questions: God, do we have ears to hear Your voice? Do we really want to hear the voice of God? In my quest for answers, I discovered that many people do not want to hear the voice of God. I discovered that most of the people from the nation of Israel made this decision after coming out of Egypt several thousands of years ago.

We read about it in Exodus 20:18-21:

Now all the people witnessed the thunderings, the lightning flashes, the sound of the trumpet, and the mountain smoking; and when the people saw it, they trembled and stood afar off. 19 Then they said to Moses, "You speak with us, and we will hear; but let not God speak with us, lest we die."

20 And Moses said to the people, "Do not fear; for God has come to test you, and that His fear may be before you, so that you may not sin." 21 So the people stood afar off, but Moses drew near the thick darkness where God was.

The first questions that we need to ask ourselves are: Do we really want to hear from God, and what are we willing to do to have that ability? In addition, would we do what He tells us to do? We can claim that in today's busy society, we just do not have the time to spend with God to hear His voice. Life is just too busy - we have to go to work - take kids to school and events – life is go, go, go and do, do, do.

These are probably similar to the same excuses that our ancestors used in times past. The crops are in the field and the sheep need tending. Life has not changed. Yet, it was hearing the voice of God that changed my life profoundly and changed the lives of countless others in the Bible.

The very first time that I heard His voice was the day I became "born again." The Bible tells us in 1 Thessalonians 2:11-12:

> *as you know how we exhorted, and comforted, and charged every one of you, as a father does his own children, 12 that you would walk worthy of God who calls you into His own kingdom and glory.*

The word *"calls"* is from the Greek word *kaleo* (kal-eh'-o). *Kaleo* (kal-eh'-o) comes from another Greek word, *kello* which means, "to urge on, hail, or incite by word" (Strong's). God calls us into His Kingdom. This means that everyone who comes to God must first hear His voice. Jesus tells us in John 3:5-8:

> *Jesus answered, "Most assuredly, I say to you, unless one is born of water and the Spirit, he cannot enter the kingdom of God. 6 That which is born of the flesh is*

flesh, and that which is born of the Spirit is spirit. 7 Do not marvel that I said to you, 'You must be born again.' 8 The wind blows where it wishes, and you hear the sound of it, but cannot tell where it comes from and where it goes. So is everyone who is born of the Spirit."

No one comes to God unless the Spirit calls him or her to God. This may prompt many people to ask the question, 'Are we predestined to salvation'? No! This is not what this means. What it means is that God knows the thoughts and intents of your heart. He will call you only when your heart is in a position to hear the Holy Spirit calling. This applies to your entire walk with God - from the moment you are born again through the rest of your life on earth. You alone are the one who puts your heart in a position to hear the voice of God. Jesus made an inquisitive statement to His followers several times: **"He who has ears to hear, let him hear!"** Jesus knew that their hearts were not in a position to hear what the Holy Spirit was saying. We see an example of this in Mark 4:2-9:

Then He taught them many things by parables, and said to them in His teaching:

3 "Listen! Behold, a sower went out to sow. 4 And it happened, as he sowed, that some seed fell by the wayside; and the birds of the air came and devoured it. 5 Some fell on stony ground, where it did not have much earth; and immediately it sprang up because it had no depth of earth. 6 But when the sun was up it was scorched, and because it had no root it withered away. 7 And some seed fell among thorns; and the thorns grew up and choked it, and it yielded no crop. 8 But other seed fell on good ground and yielded a crop that sprang up, increased and produced: some *thirtyfold, some sixty, and some a hundred." 9 And He said to them, **"He who has ears to hear, let him hear!"***

How many times in our lives do we call out to God, seeking direction: 'God, tell me what to do. Lord, I look for Your direction in my life, but yet I hear nothing.' Nevertheless, Jesus tells us in John 10:27,

"My sheep hear My voice, and I know them, and they follow Me."

In John 10:1-6, Jesus also declares:

"Most assuredly, I say to you, he who does not enter the sheepfold by the door, but climbs up some other way, the same is a thief and a robber. 2 But he who enters by the door is the shepherd of the sheep. 3 To him the doorkeeper opens, and the sheep hear his voice; and he calls his own sheep by name and leads them out. 4 And when he brings out his own sheep, he goes before them; and the sheep follow him, for they know his voice. 5 Yet they will by no means follow a stranger, but will flee from him, for they do not know the voice of strangers." 6 Jesus used this illustration, but they did not understand the things which He spoke to them.

Therefore, the question is not: 'Does God talk to us; but rather do we have ears to hear?' This is why so many Christians do not hear the voice of God. This explains what Jesus was saying in Mark 4:13 when He said, *"Do you not understand this parable? How then will you understand all the parables?*

In the parable of the sower, we understand that the seed is the word of God. However, an important part of the parable is the type of seed sown and condition of the soil upon which the seed is sown. What is the heart condition of the man hearing the word of God? Why, you may ask? God usually speaks to the heart of man, not to his physical ears.

This is the primary problem for people today. We are all listening for the voice of God through our physical ears rather than in our hearts...the location of our spiritual ears. This helps us understand why Jesus explained the parable of the sower in this way. Let us examine that whole passage again.

He began to teach again by the sea. And such a very large crowd gathered to Him that He got into a boat in the sea and sat down; and the whole crowd was by the sea on the land. 2 And He was teaching them many things in parables, and was saying to them in His teaching,

3 "Listen to this! Behold, the sower went out to sow; 4 as he was sowing, some seed fell beside the road, and the birds came and ate it up. 5 "Other seed fell on the rocky ground where it did not have much soil; and immediately it sprang up because it had no depth of soil. 6 "And after the sun had risen, it was scorched; and because it had no root, it withered away. 7 "Other seed fell among the thorns, and the thorns came up and choked it, and it yielded no crop. 8 "Other seeds fell into the good soil, and as they grew up and increased, they yielded a crop and produced thirty, sixty, and a hundredfold." 9 And He was saying, "He who has ears to hear, let him hear."

10 As soon as He was alone, His followers, along with the twelve, began asking Him about the parables. 11

And He was saying to them, "To you has been given the mystery of the kingdom of God, but those who are outside get everything in parables, 12 so that WHILE SEEING, THEY MAY SEE AND NOT PERCEIVE, AND WHILE HEARING, THEY MAY HEAR AND NOT UNDERSTAND, OTHERWISE THEY MIGHT RETURN AND BE FORGIVEN."

13 And He said to them, "Do you not understand this parable? How will you understand all the parables? 14 "The sower sows the word. 15 "These are the ones who are beside the road where the word is sown; and when they hear, immediately Satan comes and takes away the word which has been sown in them.

16 "In a similar way these are the ones on whom seed was sown on the rocky places, who, when they hear the word, immediately receive it with joy; 17 and they have no firm root in themselves, but are only temporary; then, when affliction or persecution arises because of the word, immediately they fall away. 18 "And others are the ones on whom seed was sown among the thorns; these are the ones who have heard the word, 19 but the worries of the world, and the deceitfulness of riches, and the desires for other things enter in and choke the word, and it becomes unfruitful.

20 "And those are the ones on whom seed was sown on the good soil; and they hear the word and accept it and bear fruit, thirty, sixty, and a hundredfold." Mark 4:1-20 NASU

It is quite clear, when we read this passage that man's heart can be in any one of the following four conditions at any given time. However, many people will live in one of these heart conditions their entire life. Therefore, it is important that we explore these four heart conditions of man:

THE WAYSIDE OR CARE-LESS HEART

The first heart condition we see is the wayside heart, or we can call it the care-less heart (those who could care-less about anything from God). This is a heart deceived by Satan and does not care about anything but itself, and sometimes not even itself. This type of heart condition thinks life is too short to be involved with the mundane things of God, or even believe there is a God. They believe life revolves around themselves and they see no farther than what their five physical senses convey to them.

Their lives are often focused on their inward feelings and emotions, looking for what brings them pleasure and satisfaction for the moment. Pride is the primary root of their heart condition. This makes them easy targets for Satan's deceptions. When they hear the word of God, it is easily dismissed as a fable. The sad result for this type of heart condition is most often, a life of regrets, with should-have, would-have, and could-have memories; often blaming others for missed opportunities.

One does not have to have success in life and possess many things to have a prideful heart. Pride has a taproot of self-centeredness, and is often revealed by the word "I" used countless times in a one-sided conversation.

THE STONY HEART

The second heart condition is the stony-ground heart. People with this heart condition have been hardened by life in this fallen world. Their perception in life is that some people get good breaks, and others get bad breaks. Success in life is all about luck. They believe that they are the ones who get all the bad breaks in this world. When they hear the Word of God, it sounds good for the moment. However, when tribulations come for the word's sake, they fall back to their old standard of thinking: If life is so peachy, why is it that I always get the pits? As their hearts have become hardened or calloused, they see life only through a glass half-empty perspective. Difficulties are never seen as opportunities, but only a roadblock to their happiness.

THE THORNY HEART

The third heart condition is the thorny heart. As I read this passage, I was reminded of times in my childhood when my brothers and I would go out into the blackberry patches to pick berries for our mother to make a cobbler pie. These cobblers were the best cobblers you ever tasted in your life, but in order to enjoy the fruit of our labor there was always a price to pay; as the bushes were full of thorns. The trick was to pick the berries without having our skin torn from our body by the thorns. However, often they would ensnare us as we pressed in to obtain the fruit.

In this analogy, I would compare the berries to the fruit of God's word...His promises that can produce successes in our lives. The thorns are the cares of the world, the deceitfulness

10

of riches, and the desires for other things that we must all face. They are the cares of life that will stick you whether you are successful, or not successful in life. In essence, you can own nothing and still have a thorny heart.

The thorny heart is driven by the lust of the flesh, and we know that the flesh is never satisfied. What is new today becomes old tomorrow. It is a good thing to obtain the blessings of God, but too often, when we obtain the blessings, we become snared by them. We become so enamored with the blessings, that we forget from whom and where the blessings flow. This brings us to the fourth heart condition:

THE GOOD HEART

This heart produces fruit...some thirty, some sixty, and some a hundred-fold. However, remember that sometimes our heart condition can change.

As stated previously, some people live in one of these heart conditions all their lives, while others just touch these conditions from time to time in life. Note what Jesus said about the good heart (good soil): "*But these are the ones sown on good ground, those who hear the word, accept it, and bear fruit: some thirtyfold, some sixty, and some a hundred.*" **They first must hear the word**, then they must **accept the word**, and finally, they bear fruit.

The word "*and*" is also translated as *therefore.* That means this passage can also read this way:

But these are the ones sown on good ground, those who hear the word, accept it, therefore bear fruit: some thirtyfold, some sixty, and some a hundred."

Note, the first requirement is to hear the word of God. The word, *"hear"* is translated from the Greek word *akouo,* which means, "to hear in various senses", but also includes "to comprehend or understand" (Thayer's).

Next, the good heart accepts the word. *"Accept"* comes from the Greek word, *paradechomai,* connoting "to accept near", or "to receive the word". However, after you accept it, the word should produce results - and the results should be that of bearing fruit.

The word, *"bear"* comes from the Greek word *karpophoreo,* which means, "to be fertile" (literally or figuratively), or "bring forth fruit". This word connotes an action on our part. It is this action on the word, that produces thirty, sixty, and one hundred-fold returns on God's promises in our life. Man always produces a fruit based on what he believes, for *"as he thinks in his heart, so he is "*(Pr. 23:7).

The key to this passage is not the action on our part, but the comprehension and understanding of the word that we have received. Without the correct understanding, our action may be completely wrong. Our motives or intentions may be good, but our actions may produce the wrong fruit because of misunderstanding.

How many times in our life have we received the fruits of something we have done based on a wrong decision? The Bible gives us a great example of this in the Book of Acts. Starting in chapter eight, we can read about a young man by the name of

Saul. This young man had a great zeal for God. Based on his understanding of God and scripture, he acted on what he believed; even to the point of having Christians stoned to death.

It was not until Acts chapter nine that we read about Saul having an encounter with Christ, which changed his flawed understanding, and put an end to his destructive fruits. It was from this point forward that his new understanding would produce a different fruit. Saul, now known as Paul, writes about the importance of gaining understanding in his letter to the church at Ephesus:

> *For this reason, because I have heard of your faith in the Lord Jesus and your love toward all the saints (the people of God), 16 I do not cease to give thanks for you, making mention of you in my prayers. 17[For I always pray to] the God of our Lord Jesus Christ, the Father of glory, that He may grant you a spirit of wisdom and revelation [of insight into mysteries and secrets] in the [deep and intimate] knowledge of Him,*
>
> *18 By having the eyes of your heart flooded with light, so that you can know and understand the hope to which He has called you, and how rich is His glorious inheritance in the saints (His set-apart ones),* Eph.1:15-18 AMP

The Apostle Paul learned that **spiritual understanding** comes only one way...through revelation given by the Holy Spirit of God.

CHAPTER 2

WORDS AND THE CIRCLE OF LIFE

One of the greatest blessings of life is becoming a parent. Nevertheless, as time passes and we grow older, we sometimes forget many of the little things that we experience through our children. However, when the grandchildren arrive, you re-live and remember some of those blessings; such as their first words.

For the first year or so, communication is difficult. We understand nothing that the baby is saying. Its language skills are limited or nonexistent. Not only do we not understand it, but neither does it understand us...so communication is difficult. It is only through time spent with the child that it learns to understand our language and to communicate with us. This issue is no different for us today, as we desire to communicate with God.

Jesus tells us in John 3:3, that in order for us to enter the Kingdom of God, *"we must be born again"*. This statement not only reveals the method by which we are required to enter relationship with God, but it also gives us insight as to what to expect after we enter that relationship. Just as a newborn baby comes into this physical world, and has to learn to communicate, we go through the same process again when we enter the Kingdom of God as a newborn spiritual person.

The Kingdom of God operates in the spiritual realm, or a different dimension. As stated previously, Jesus often made this inquisitive statement to His followers: *"He who has ears to hear, let him hear!""*? They were trying to gain spiritual understanding with physical eyes and ears. This is why Jesus made the statement in Matthew 13:13:

> *"Therefore I speak to them in parables, **because seeing they do not see, and hearing they do not hear, nor do they understand.**"*

It is only when we understand that we must learn to communicate in the spiritual realm, if we are to obtain our goal of hearing the voice of God. Is God talking to you? Yes, but the real question is: Do you have ears to hear - or even more importantly, do you want to hear the voice of God? I believe the answer to these questions rests in the fact that you are reading this book.

The very first step in our learning process is to understand that God does not force Himself on anyone. God will call you, but you have to make the decision to respond or reply. God has supplied a method by which we can enter relationship with Him through His covenant of Grace...the free gift of adoption into His family. This opportunity to receive Grace is made available to everyone who recognizes that all people have sinned and fallen short of the glory of God. This includes you and me.

> *But now apart from the Law the righteousness of God has been manifested, being witnessed by the Law and the Prophets, 22 even the righteousness of God through faith in Jesus Christ for all those who believe; for there is no distinction; 23 **for all have sinned and fall short of the glory***

of God, *24 being justified as a gift by His grace through the redemption which is in Christ Jesus; 25 whom God displayed publicly as a propitiation in His blood through faith.* Rom 3:21-25 NASU

It is only when we come to the cross of Jesus Christ, God's only begotten son, and receive by faith His death as payment for our sin, that we can enter a covenant relationship with the righteous God. If you do not seek to know God, His method is meaningless to you. However, if you truly seek to know Him, you will hear His voice for the first time when He calls you.

Jesus tells us in John 6:44-45;

No one can come to Me unless the Father who sent Me draws him; *and I will raise him up at the last day.*

The question is often asked: Why does God not talk to everyone all the time? The answer being, sin separates man from God. God being righteous, does not fellowship with unrighteousness. This unrighteous state of being, or living, actually places man in a position of spiritual death. The literal meaning of *death* is defined as "being separated from" (Webster). When we die physically, our spirit separates from our body. The physical body loses the vitality of life that it derives from the spirit. We are a spirit that lives in a body and has a soul. In the same manner, spiritual death means we are separated from God, because our spirit derives its life from God. Sin produces spiritual death by separating us from God. This will be the final great judgment...eternal separation from God, producing eternal spiritual death.

However, God has presented to us a way for the spirit to be restored, or resurrected from spiritual death to spiritual life with Him. We, by faith, receive His covenant of Grace. How we do that is best defined in Romans 10:6-13:

> *But the righteousness of faith speaks in this way, "Do not say in your heart, 'Who will ascend into heaven?'" (that is, to bring Christ down from above) 7 or, "'Who will descend into the abyss?'" (that is, to bring Christ up from the dead).*
>
> *8 But what does it say? "The word is near you, in your mouth and in your heart" (that is, the word of faith which we preach): 9 that if you confess with your mouth the Lord Jesus and believe in your heart that God has raised Him from the dead, you will be saved. 10 For with the heart one believes unto righteousness, and with the mouth confession is made unto salvation.*
>
> *11 For the Scripture says, "Whoever believes on Him will not be put to shame." 12 For there is no distinction between Jew and Greek, for the same Lord over all is rich to all who call upon Him. 13 For "whoever calls on the name of the LORD shall be saved."*

As you read in this passage, believing is just one part of the process of salvation. The other part involves the words that we confess with our mouths. We have previously discussed the type of heart condition required for obtaining fellowship with God, but Jesus makes a profound statement that we find recorded in Matthew 12:34-35:

> *"For out of the **abundance** of the heart the mouth speaks. 35 A good man out of the good treasure of his heart brings forth good things, and an evil man out of the evil treasure brings forth evil things."*

The word *"abundance"*, Matthew penned here, comes from the Greek word *perisseuma*. It can translate two ways: "something in which one delights" or "what is left over, residue, or remains" (Thayer's). I believe it is best described as an overflow of what we have put into our hearts.

We can guard our mouths closely, but eventually words will reveal what we have filled our hearts with, and what we believe or delight in will overflow out of our mouths. In essence, the word that proceed from our mouth are the product of what seed we have planted in our heart.

Therefore, we can best describe our heart, as a garden. And what we plant in our garden (heart) as a seed. This seed will produce after its own kind. What does it produce? It produces words that proceed from our mouth, and they become seed to the heart of those who hear them. This I call, **'the circle of life'**.

When we examine the circle of life, I am reminded of the proverbial question: Which came first, the chicken or the egg... the chicken being the fruit of seed that was planted in the egg. However, if we do not have the chicken, we have no egg or seed to produce the chicken. You know the point. This is not the case with God's creation. We read in John 1:1-5;

> *In the beginning was the Word, and the Word was with God, and the Word was God. 2 He was in the beginning with God. 3 All things were made through Him, and without Him nothing was made that was made. 4 In Him was life, and the life was the light of men. 5 And the light shines in the darkness, and the darkness did not comprehend it.*

As we just read, all of creation had a beginning. It started with God's spoken word. We read in Hebrews 11:3;

By faith we understand that the worlds were framed by the word of God, so that the things which are seen were not made of things which are visible.

Moreover, in Romans chapter four, verse seventeen, we discover that God, *"calls those things which do not exist as though they did"* (NKJV).

All of creation came into existence when God **called,** or spoke it into existence, with the exception of man. Man was not called into existence. We read the account of man's creation in Genesis 1:26-28:

*Then God said, **"Let Us make man in Our image**, according to Our likeness; let them have dominion over the fish of the sea, over the birds of the air, and over the cattle, over all the earth and over every creeping thing that creeps on the earth."*

27 So God created man in His own image; in the image of God He created him; male and female He created them. 28 Then God blessed them, and God said to them, "Be fruitful and multiply; fill the earth and subdue it; have dominion over the fish of the sea, over the birds of the air, and over every living thing that moves on the earth."

As we note, God spoke into being everything He planned for creation, but He did not call man into existence. Rather, He formed man from the dust of the ground and breathed into his nostrils the breath of life; thus, man became a living being (Gen. 2:7). This means man is unique from all the rest of creation, because **God made man with His hands...not with words, but with touch**.

We can read many passages in the Bible about Jesus touching or being touched, by people. Many times, it was for healings to take place in their bodies. We read also in Mark 16:17-18 that Jesus instructed us to do the same:

"And these signs will follow those who believe: In My name they will cast out demons; they will speak with new tongues; 18 they will take up serpents; and if they drink anything deadly, it will by no means hurt them; **they will lay hands on the sick, and they will recover."**

God said, *"Let Us* **make** *man in Our* **image.**" The word, *make,* means to fashion in the sense of squeezing something into shape. Vine's defines the word *"image"* as a copy of something in the sense of a replica. Does this mean that when we see man, we see what God looks like? No! I believe Jesus answered this question in John 14:9-11:

Jesus said to him, "Have I been with you so long, and yet you have not known Me, Philip? He who has seen Me has seen the Father; so how can you say, 'Show us the Father'? 10 Do you not believe that I am in the Father, and the Father in Me? The words that I speak to you I do not speak on My own authority; but the Father who dwells in Me does the works.

11 Believe Me that I am in the Father and the Father in Me, or else believe Me for the sake of the works themselves."

From this explanation to Philip, we understand that the image of God is Spirit and cannot be seen by the human eye. This word *"image",* or replica, is really giving us the understanding of the Godhead: The Father (God), the Son (Jesus), and the Holy Spirit...the three parts that make the whole of the Godhead. Man is a replica of the Godhead - the spirit, the body, and the soul; three in one, just as the Godhead is three in one.

It is important for us to understand what this word *"image"* means, as I believe we often miss the most important point of man being a replica of the Godhead. In ancient Hebrew, a name or word, would not only identify, but also define its function. Therefore, a replica should also function or operate as the original operates. How does God operate? He calls things into existence with words empowered by faith.

As we have seen, all of creation came into being by God calling it into existence. This is why the Bible goes to great lengths to teach us the power of our words. Jesus gave this instruction to His Disciples in Mark 11:22-25:

> *"Have faith in God. 23 " Truly I say to you, **whoever says** to this mountain, 'Be taken up and cast into the sea,' and **does not doubt in his heart, but believes that what he says is going to happen, it will be granted him.** 24 "Therefore I say to you, all things for which you pray and ask, believe that you have received them, and they will be granted you."* NASU

CHAPTER 3

POWER OF THE TONGUE

My brethren, let not many of you become teachers, knowing that we shall receive a stricter judgment. 2 For we all stumble in many things. **If anyone does not stumble in word, he is a perfect man, able also to bridle the whole body.** *3 Indeed, we put bits in horses' mouths that they may obey us, and we turn their whole body.*

4 Look also at ships: although they are so large and are driven by fierce winds, they are turned by a very small rudder wherever the pilot desires. 5 Even so the tongue is a little member and boasts great things. See how great a forest a little fire kindles! 6 And the tongue is a fire, a world of iniquity. **The tongue is so set among our members that it defiles the whole body, and sets on fire the course of nature; and it is set on fire by hell.**

7 For every kind of beast and bird, of reptile and creature of the sea, is tamed and has been tamed by mankind. 8 But no man can tame the tongue. It is an unruly evil, full of deadly poison. 9 With it we bless our God and Father, and with it we curse men, who have been made in the similitude of God. 10 Out of the same mouth proceed blessing and cursing. My brethren, these things ought not to be so.

11 Does a spring send forth fresh water and bitter from the same opening? 12 Can a fig tree, my brethren, bear olives, or a grapevine bear figs? Thus no spring yields both salt water and fresh. James 3:1-13

As we discussed in the previous chapter, God created man in His image (Gen. 1:26). When we examine man, we not only see that man is a spirit, soul, and body, just as the Godhead, but we should live our lives in the same manner as God (Eph 5:1 *Therefore be imitators of God, as beloved children.*).

The Apostle James gave us insight into this truth by explaining the power of the tongue in our lives. The tongue can defile the whole body and set on fire the course of nature. The Greek word translated as *"nature"* is the word *genesis*. The word *genesis* means "beginning or origin" and originates from the Greek root word *ginomai*, which means, "to cause to happen, come to pass, or be fulfilled" (Strong's).

The words that proceed from our mouth are seeds, and a creative force. They are carried on the wind of our breath. Words will cause things to happen. Just as God's word is seed and was, and still is, a creative force and brought everything into existence, your words work the same way. They are a creative force in your life, and the lives of those around you.

That is why Proverbs chapter eighteen, verse twenty-one, tells us that **death and life are in the power of the tongue, And those who love it will eat its fruit.**

You will eat the fruit of what your mouth produces…life or death. Jesus gives us great insight into this truth, as we read again His statement in Mark 11:22-24:

So Jesus answered and said to them, "Have faith in God. 23 For assuredly, I say to you, whoever says to this mountain, 'Be removed and be cast into the sea,' and does not doubt in his heart, but believes that those things he says will be done, he will have whatever he says. 24 Therefore I say to you, whatever things you ask when you pray, believe that you receive them, and you will have them."

Jesus said, *"whoever says to this mountain"* and *"believes in his heart."* *"Whoever"* applies to anyone who speaks to mountains or obstacles in life, and believes what he says will come to pass. He will see the results, the fruit of what he believes. This is faith in action...a faith that calls those things that do not exist in the physical world as though they do. Again, this is exactly what God did when He created everything. We see this in Hebrews 11:3:

By faith we understand that the worlds were framed by the word of God, so that the things which are seen were not made of things which are visible.

We read this truth again in Rom. 4:17:

God, who gives life to the dead and calls those things which do not exist as though they did;

God envisioned in His imagination what the world would be, and then spoke it into existence. Why is this so important to us? As discussed earlier, you and I are created in the image of God. We are to live our lives mimicking what our creator, God, did. This is what the Apostle Paul tells us in First Corinthians chapter eleven, verse one, **"Imitate me, just as I also imitate Christ".**

What did Jesus do? Jesus spoke, believed, and received, all in faith. Therefore, (by faith) we should also speak what we want to see manifested in our lives, and in our families.

25

I have witnessed this truth in my life and in countless other lives. At the age of thirty, I started confessing that I would be retired from business and working in full-time ministry at the age of fifty. At the age of fifty, I retired from business and began full-time ministry.

I cannot tell you how many times I have witnessed people make statements about their lives that later came to pass. Most often, their words were derived from fear, and because it motivated their beliefs, what they spoke is what they received. But fear should not be our motivator, but rather faith in God's word.

THE LAW OF SOWING AND REAPING

Why do words have such power? Our words became powerful when God established **the creation law of sowing and reaping** in Genesis 1:11-20:

Then God said, "Let the earth bring forth grass, the herb that yields seed, and the fruit tree that yields fruit according to its kind, whose seed is in itself, on the earth"; and it was so. 12 And the earth brought forth grass, the herb that yields seed according to its kind, and the tree that yields fruit, whose seed is in itself according to its kind. And God saw that it was good. 13 So the evening and the morning were the third day.

14 Then God said, "Let there be lights in the firmament of the heavens to divide the day from the night; and let them be for signs and seasons, and for days and years; 15 and let them be for lights in the firmament of the heavens to give light on the earth"; and it was so. 16

Then God made two great lights: the greater light to rule the day, and the lesser light to rule the night. He made the stars also. 17 God set them in the firmament of the heavens to give light on the earth, 18 and to rule over the day and over the night, and to divide the light from the darkness. And God saw that it was good. 19 So the evening and the morning were the fourth day.

20 Then God said, "Let the waters abound with an abundance of living creatures, and let birds fly above the earth across the face of the firmament of the heavens." 21 So God created great sea creatures and every living thing that moves, with which the waters abounded, according to their kind, and every winged bird according to its kind. And God saw that it was good. 22 And God blessed them, saying, "Be fruitful and multiply, and fill the waters in the seas, and let birds multiply on the earth." 23 So the evening and the morning were the fifth day.

Everything shall produce after its own kind. The Apostle Paul tells us in Galatians 6:7-9:

*Do not be deceived, God is not mocked; for **whatever a man sows, that he will also reap**. 8 For he who sows to his flesh will of the flesh reap corruption, but he who sows to the Spirit will of the Spirit reap everlasting life. 9 And let us not grow weary while doing good, for in due season we shall reap if we do not lose heart.*

In this statement, we see that we have the opportunity to sow either to our flesh or to our spirit. Whatever words we sow, produces one or the other - life or death.

Why do I call it a creation law? We have been redeemed from the curse of the law by the works of the cross. But there are creation laws, if broken, from which we have not been redeemed. Creation laws apply to many of the laws of physics. For example, we have knowledge of the creation law of gravity. What goes up will come down. The only way to overcome the law of gravity is by the law of force and lift. We see this every day when an airplane flies overhead (Newton's Law of Lift).

However, if we remove the wings and engines that provide the force and lift, that airplane will no longer alter the law of gravity, and it will remain on the ground. These are creation laws, which we call laws of physics. Jesus tells us about the creation law of words, as we read again the parable of the sower:

*And He said to them, "Do you not understand this parable? How then will you understand all the parables? 14 **The sower sows the word.** 15 And these are the ones by the wayside where the word is sown. When they hear, Satan comes immediately and takes away the word that was sown in their hearts.*

16 These likewise are the ones sown on stony ground who, when they hear the word, immediately receive it with gladness; 17 and they have no root in themselves, and so endure only for a time. Afterward, when tribulation or persecution arises for the word's sake, immediately they stumble.

18 Now these are the ones sown among thorns; they are the ones who hear the word, 19 and the cares of this world, the deceitfulness of riches, and the desires for other things entering in choke the word, and it becomes unfruitful. 20 But these are the ones sown on good ground, those who hear the word, accept it, and bear fruit: some thirtyfold, some sixty, and some a hundred." Mark 4:13-20

As Jesus explains, words produce a fruit and a return: some thirty-fold, some sixty, and some a hundred-fold return. If we do not understand how words affect our lives in this world, we will not understand how God created this world to operate. Thus, we will suffer loss in this life for the lack of knowledge. **However, words by themselves produce nothing until they are mixed with what we believe in our heart (faith)**. Jesus explains this truth very clearly in Matt 12:34-37, and its repercussions.

> *"For the mouth speaks out of that which fills the heart. 35 "The good man brings out of his good treasure what is good; and the evil man brings out of his evil treasure what is evil. 36 "But I tell you that every careless word that people speak, they shall give an accounting for it in the Day of Judgment. 37 "**For by your words you will be justified, and by your words you will be condemned.**"*
> NASU

Do we believe God at His word, or do we believe the world and the fears it can produce in us? This brings us to a very important point of understanding about faith. Now, let us consider a simple definition of this thing called *"faith".*

Faith, in its simplest form, is what we believe in our hearts to be true. The Old Covenant Hebrew most often uses the word 'aman (aw-man'), a primitive root word, instead of the word faith. 'Aman, connotes the mind set of trust, or to believe properly; to build up or support; to be true or certain; to stand firm; to trust or put faith in someone or something. What we believe in our hearts inspires the words we speak and motivates the actions we take in life.

Now let us also consider fear. Most people would define fear as that which imposes dread of failure, or defeat and loss. Many believe fear to be the opposite of faith, thinking it stands in direct opposition to faith. Is that a true understanding?

If faith is what we believe in our hearts to be true, and if what we believe in our heart is fear based, then what is the fruit produced? What do I mean by that question? Let us consider these passages of Scripture in Rom 12:3-4:

> *For I say, through the grace given to me, to everyone who is among you, not to think of himself more highly than he ought to think, but to think soberly, as **God has dealt to each one a measure of faith**.*

2 Tim 1:7

> **For God has not given us a spirit of fear**, *but of power and of love and of a sound mind.*

Through these passages, we understand that faith is given by God, and fear is not from God. It is important that we remember that **faith is simply the ability to believe, as it is a gift from God**. If faith is simply believing, then faith is neutral until it is influenced by a truth, or a lie.

Now some may point out, but Brother Rod, what does Hebrews 11:1 say? It says: *Now faith is the substance of things hoped for, the evidence of things not seen* (NKJV). If faith is the substance of things hoped for, surely no one is hoping for their fears to come to pass, are they? That is a good question. However, when we consider that the word, *hoped*, comes from the Greek word, elpizo (el-pid'-zo), we discover that its definition is: **Expectation - whether of good or bad** (Thayer's).

Let us consider it this way: If someone has fear grip their heart (faith focused on what they fear) and speaks what they believe, the odds are very high that they will get what they believe. What they believe in their heart to be a perceived truth, and by the creative power of faith, it can come into existence. Is it any wonder that the Apostle Paul tells to us to, *"be anxious for nothing"* (Phil 4:6).

Then, as we read Peter's message about anxiety, he tells us to, *"cast all your anxiety on Him (Jesus), because He cares for you* (1 Peter 5:6-8) NASU. Proverbs gives us additional insight about the effects produced by fear, in Prov 12:25;

> *Anxiety in a man's heart weighs it down, But a good word makes it glad.* NASU

"Anxiety" comes from the Hebrew word, de'agah (deh-aw-gaw'), which connotes the idea of **fear,** heaviness, or sorrow. In essence, fear is the fruit of believing (having faith) in our heart for things that are contrary to God's truth. We hear this truth from Job (3:25): *"For **what I fear comes upon me,** And what I dread befalls me* (NASU). Jesus also addressed this issue directly in several instances.

Luke 8:49-55

> *While He was still speaking, someone came from the house of the synagogue official, saying, "**Your daughter has died;** do not trouble the Teacher anymore." 50 But when Jesus heard this, He answered him, "**Do not be afraid any longer; only believe,** and she will be made well."*

31

51 When He came to the house, He did not allow anyone to enter with Him, except Peter and John and James, and the girl's father and mother. 52 Now they were all weeping and lamenting for her; but He said, "Stop weeping, for she has not died, but is asleep."

*53 And they began laughing at Him, knowing that she had died. 54 He, however, took her by the hand and called, saying, "Child, arise!" 55 And **her spirit returned, and she got up immediately;** and He gave orders for something to be given her to eat.* NASU

Mark 11:20-24

*As they were passing by in the morning, they saw the fig tree withered from the roots up. 21 Being reminded, Peter said to Him, "Rabbi, look, the fig tree which You cursed has withered." 22 And Jesus answered saying to them, "**Have faith in God.** 23" Truly I say to you, whoever says to this mountain, 'Be taken up and cast into the sea,' and **does not doubt in his heart, but believes** that what he says is going to happen, it will be granted him."* NASU

Mark 9:20-28

*They brought the boy to Him. When he saw Him, immediately the spirit threw him into a convulsion, and falling to the ground, he began rolling around and foaming at the mouth. 21 And He asked his father, "How long has this been happening to him?" And he said, "From childhood. 22 "It has often thrown him both into the fire and into the water to destroy him. But **if You can do anything,** take pity on us and help us!"*

*23 And Jesus said to him, "'If You can?' **All things are possible to him who believes**." 24 Immediately the boy's father cried out and said, **"I do believe; help my unbelief."** 25 When Jesus saw that a crowd was rapidly gathering, He rebuked the unclean spirit, saying to it, "You deaf and mute spirit, I command you, come out of him and do not enter him again."*

26 After crying out and throwing him into terrible convulsions, it came out; and the boy became so much like a corpse that most of them said, "He is dead!" 27 But Jesus took him by the hand and raised him; and he got up. NASU

Lastly, we see no better example of this than when someone comes to Jesus for salvation. They hear the Gospel of Truth, and **they believe it in their hearts and confess it with their mouths - producing the fruit of salvation** (Romans 10:10). However, no one comes to God unless **he or she hears the voice of the Holy Spirit calling them.**

Unless we have ears to hear, we will not recognize the voice of God when He speaks to us. The first thing every Christian should learn is to pray for the eyes and ears of understanding for those that are lost to be opened, so that they will hear the voice of God calling them, to come to Him. The Lord spoke this in Ezekiel 12:1-2:

Now the word of the LORD came to me, saying: 2 "Son of man, you dwell in the midst of a rebellious house, which has eyes to see but does not see, and ears to hear but does not hear; for they are a rebellious house.

When anyone first comes to God, it is by hearing the call of the Holy Spirit. Jesus tells us in John 8:47, "*He who is of God*

33

hears God's words (RHEMA – which we will define later in this book).

He goes on to say in John 10:1-5:

*"Most assuredly, I say to you, he who does not enter the sheepfold by the door, but climbs up some other way, the same is a thief and a robber. 2 But he who enters by the door is the shepherd of the sheep. 3 To him the doorkeeper opens, and **the sheep hear his voice;** and he calls his own sheep by name and leads them out.*

*4 And when he brings out his own sheep, he goes before them; and the sheep follow him, for **they know his voice.** 5 Yet they will by no means follow a stranger, but will flee from him, for **they do not know the voice of strangers."***

In verse four, Jesus said, *"They know his voice,"* in reference to the shepherd. The sheep know and understand, or comprehend, the shepherd's voice. Then Jesus also tells us in John 16:12-14:

*"I still have many things to say to you, but you cannot bear them now. 13 However, when He, the Spirit of truth, has come, He will guide you into all truth; for He will not speak on His own authority, but whatever He hears He will speak; and He will **tell** you things to come."*

So, if God is talking to His people today, how does He do it and how do we, His people, have ears to hear? Moreover, why is it so important for you and I to hear the voice of God? We obtain some understanding of this in Mark 4:21-25:

Also He said to them, "Is a lamp brought to be put under a basket or under a bed? Is it not to be set on a lamp stand? 22 For there is nothing hidden which will not be revealed, nor has anything been kept secret but that it should come to light.

*23 If anyone has ears to hear, let him hear." 24 Then He said to them, **"Take heed what you hear.** With the same measure you use, it will be measured to you; and to you who hear, more will be given. 25 For whoever has, to him more will be given; but whoever does not have, even what he has will be taken away from him."*

Jesus said for us to, *"take heed to what you hear."* This is an important statement - as we will discover later that there are many voices speaking to us, and not all are good. He goes on to say, "to those who hear, more will be given. And for those who do not hear, even what they have will be lost."

Many Christians suffer loss and defeat because they do not recognize the voice of God. God tells them to do one thing, and because they do not hear, they do not obey. However, we should remember it is God who **always** leads us in triumph in Christ (2 Cor. 2:14). If God **always** leads us in triumph, then we also need to recognize who leads us into failure, loss, and defeat. For the one who is led into failure will suffer loss. We need to understand that there is an enemy to the Church, and that he is still speaking and deceiving today. Jesus tells us in John 10:10;

"The thief does not come except to steal, and to kill, and to destroy. I have come that they may have life and that they may have it more abundantly."

Over the next several chapters, we will examine the ways God communicated with His people in history, and see that God has not changed His ways in six-thousand years.

CHAPTER 4

DOES GOD COMMUNICATE WITH PEOPLE?

The first answer to this question is obvious. There are many times in history when God spoke directly to His people. Adam talked to God directly in the Garden of Eden. Abraham talked to God in the presence of angels in Genesis chapter eighteen. God talked with Moses through a burning bush in Exodus chapter three. Moreover, many times Moses heard an audible voice. We can read account after account in the Old Testament of such audible events happening to men, as God was using them at the time. However, the question remains: How does God talk to His people today? To discover the answer to that question, let us first start by reading what Peter said on the Day of Pentecost:

> And _it shall come to pass in the last days_, says God, That _I will pour out of My Spirit on all flesh; Your sons and your daughters shall _prophesy_, Your young men shall _see visions_, Your old men shall _dream dreams_. 18 And on My menservants and on My maidservants I will pour out My Spirit in those days; And they shall prophesy. Acts 2:17-18

Peter was quoting here from the prophet Joel. But he was prompted to make this quote after some events had taken place that caught the whole city by surprise. While one hundred and twenty people were in prayer in an upper room, the Holy Spirit of God descended upon and into the people there. We read about the events that occur immediately afterwards in Acts 2:4-13:

> And **they were all filled with the Holy Spirit** and began to speak with other tongues, as **the Spirit gave them utterance**. 5 And there were dwelling in Jerusalem Jews, devout men, from every nation under heaven. 6 And when this sound occurred, the multitude came together, and were confused, because everyone heard them speak in his own language. 7 Then they were all amazed and marveled, saying to one another, "Look, are not all these who speak Galileans? 8 And how is it that we hear, each in our own language in which we were born?
>
> 9 Parthians and Medes and Elamites, those dwelling in Mesopotamia, Judea and Cappadocia, Pontus and Asia, 10 Phrygia and Pamphylia, Egypt and the parts of Libya adjoining Cyrene, visitors from Rome, both Jews and proselytes, 11 Cretans and Arabs — we hear them speaking in our own tongues the wonderful works of God."
>
> 12 So they were all amazed and perplexed, saying to one another, "Whatever could this mean?" 13 Others mocking said, "They are full of new wine."

Because of this event, there was great turmoil in the city. Thousands came to see what was happening that day. It became apparent that God was speaking through His people as **the Spirit gave them utterance.** It had to be such a miraculous and unique event that it prompted about three thousand people to commit their lives that day to Jesus Christ - the very man they had just witnessed crucified forty days beforehand. What these people were prophesying could have come only from God, because He spoke the same thing using so many different languages. How could they speak God's words without hearing what the Spirit was saying?

PROPHESY

This event on the day of Pentecost demonstrated God's gift of prophesy to His New Covenant Church. Throughout Old Covenant history, God used prophets to speak to His people Israel, and after this event, it is clear that He will use prophets to continue to speak to His church. However, as we will continue to discover, this is not the only way God will speak to His people.

There are many who believe that prophets and prophesy were used by God only through the disciples, and that they are no longer for the Church today. However, we need only to remember what is to happen as stated in the Book of Revelation, chapter eleven, when God uses two prophets for the end-of- time events. We also read in Ephesians 4:11-16:

*And He Himself gave some to be **apostles,** some **prophets,** some **evangelists,** and some **pastors** and **teachers,** 12 for the equipping of the saints for the work of ministry, for the edifying of the body of Christ, 13 till we all come to the unity of the faith and of the knowledge of the Son of God, to a perfect man, to the measure of the stature of the fullness of Christ; 14 that we should no longer be children, tossed to and fro and carried about with every wind of doctrine, by the trickery of men, in the cunning craftiness of deceitful plotting,*

15 but, speaking the truth in love, may grow up in all things into Him who is the head — Christ — 16 from whom the whole body, joined and knit together by what every joint supplies, according to the effective working by which every part does its share, causes growth of the body for the edifying of itself in love.

As we read this passage from Paul's letter, it becomes apparent that the Church today has not attained the level described by Paul, and that the need for all five ministry gifts are still required to bring the Church to the highest level of maturity.

All five ministry gifts, set in place by God, are required to equip the Church as He intended. Therefore, it should be obvious, that God will not remove the very gifts He has set in place to obtain His desired results for the Church.

However, as we will discover, prophesy is only one of the ways God speaks to His people, and there are dangers for those who are led only by prophets. Remember, there were many false prophets in the days of the Old Covenant, and they prophesied error.

Nonetheless, God equips us with ways to confirm what the prophets are saying, as we will discover later in this book. We should never act on the word of the prophet alone, but should seek confirmation from God.

DREAMS AND VISIONS

Another way God speaks to His people is through dreams. How many people have dreams today and fail to realize the significance of the event. Sigmund Freud believed dreams are a window into our subconscious mind. He believed they expose a person's unconscious desires, thoughts; and sometimes motivations. He also thought dreams were a way for people to placate urges and desires that were unacceptable to society. In his book "The Interpretation of Dreams", Freud wrote that dreams are "...disguised fulfillments of repressed wishes." Perhaps there is some merit with all these theories, however, scientists are still trying to figure out exactly why we dream.

I do know from personal experience that when I eat heavy fat foods late at night, I have dreams, i.e. Ice Cream. I do not know what I am repressing, other than the thought of eating all the Ice Cream I want and not gain a pound. One thing science has proven is that everyone has dreams. They may not remember them, but they are there.

In the spiritual aspect, a dream may be a warning or even a foretelling of what is to come in one's life. Many men in the Old Testament experienced dreams from God. Jacob, Joseph, Solomon, Daniel, and Joseph (Jesus' stepfather), all received words from God through dreams. Even Nebuchadnezzar, king of Babylon, had a dream for which he called upon Daniel, the man of God, to interpret.

Dan 2:1-3

Now in the second year of the reign of Nebuchadnezzar, Nebuchadnezzar had dreams; and his spirit was troubled and his sleep left him. 2 Then the king gave orders to call in the magicians, the conjurers, the sorcerers and the Chaldeans to tell the king his dreams. So they came in and stood before the king. 3

The king said to them, "I had a dream and my spirit is anxious to understand the dream." NASU

Dan 2:26-29

The king said to Daniel, whose name was Belteshazzar, "Are you able to make known to me the dream which I have seen and its interpretation?" 27 Daniel answered before the king and said, "As for the mystery about which the king has inquired, neither wise men, conjurers, magicians nor diviners are able to declare it to the king.

28 "However, there is a God in heaven who reveals mysteries, and He has made known to King Nebuchadnezzar what will take place in the latter days. This was your dream and the visions in your mind while on your bed. 29 "As for you, O king, while on your bed your thoughts turned to what would take place in the future; and He who reveals mysteries has made known to you what will take place. NASU

Dan 2:46-48

Then King Nebuchadnezzar fell on his face and did homage to Daniel, and gave orders to present to him an offering and fragrant incense. 47 The king answered Daniel and said, "Surely your God is a God of gods and a Lord of kings and a revealer of mysteries, since you have been able to reveal this mystery."

48 Then the king promoted Daniel and gave him many great gifts, and he made him ruler over the whole province of Babylon and chief prefect over all the wise men of Babylon. NASU

In the New Testament, Matthew chapter two, verse twelve, the three wise men receive a warning in a dream:

*Then, being divinely warned **in a dream** that they should not return to Herod, they departed for their own country another way.*

Visions are another way God speaks to His people. This occurred many times in the Book of Acts:

*About the ninth hour of the day he saw clearly **in a vision** an angel of God coming in and saying to him, "Cornelius!" Acts 10:3*

While Peter thought about the vision, the Spirit said to him, "Behold, three men are seeking you. 20 Arise therefore, go down and go with them, doubting nothing; for I have sent them." Acts 10:19-20

*And **a vision** appeared to Paul in the night. A man of Macedonia stood and pleaded with him, saying, "Come over to Macedonia and help us." Acts 16:9*

*Now the Lord spoke to Paul in the night **by a vision**, "Do not be afraid, but speak, and do not keep silent; 10 for I am with you, and no one will attack you to hurt you; for I have many people in this city." Acts 18:9 -11*

Therefore, we see that it was not just the Apostles Peter and Paul who received visions, but also Cornelius. The Book of Acts gives us this description of Cornelius:

There was a certain man in Caesarea called Cornelius, a centurion of what was called the Italian Regiment, 2 a devout man and one who feared God with all his household, who gave alms generously to the people, and prayed to God always. Acts 10:1-3

Whether it was an Apostle, or a Roman soldier, God was speaking to His people through visions. However, let us remember that the Apostle Paul did warn us in 2 Cor. 11:13-14:

For such are false apostles, deceitful workers, transforming themselves into apostles of Christ. 14 And no wonder! For Satan himself transforms himself into an angel of light.

Many years ago, I experienced a vision while standing in my kitchen. My wife had just left our home to take our daughter to school. As I reached for the handle of our refrigerator, a vision of an intersection flashed before my eyes. The Holy Spirit impressed upon me to pray. So I stopped everything and prayed for my wife and daughter's safety in travel. It was later that evening that my wife shared with me what happened when she was returning from picking up our daughter that afternoon. She came to that intersection, which is a four way stop, and stopped. As she started to proceed through the intersection, she felt the need to stop again. It was at that time two young men in a vehicle ran through their stop sign at a very high rate of speed. Had she not stopped the second time, the impact would have been catastrophic.

God still speaks to His people today through visions. Have we trained our eyes to see and ears to hear?

How do we discern the real from the fake? How do we recognize false prophets, demonic dreams, or Satan disguised as an angel of light? We are to use two very important armaments God has supplied to the Church - *Rhema* and

Logos. These two Greek words are the foundation of this book, and our discussion of their unique use is of extreme importance to the Church and all believers. We will examine their importance, meaning, and usage, as we proceed in future chapters.

VISITATIONS

Finally, there can be times of visitation by angels of God. We can read about these visitation events in many books of the Old Testament, (Adam – Gen 3) (Noah – Gen 6) (Abraham – Gen 18) (Moses – Ex 3) (Joshua – Josh 5), but there are several events in the New Testament in which we find God speaking to His people this way.

Then the high priest rose up, and all those who were with him (which is the sect of the Sadducees), and they were filled with indignation, 18 and laid their hands on the apostles and put them in the common prison.

*19 But at night **an angel of the Lord** opened the prison doors and brought them out, and said, 20 "Go, stand in the temple and speak to the people all the words of this life." 21 And when they heard that, they entered the temple early in the morning and taught.* Acts 5:17-21

We find two additional events also in Acts:

Peter was therefore kept in prison, but constant prayer was offered to God for him by the church. 6 And when Herod was about to bring him out, that night Peter was sleeping, bound with two chains between two soldiers; and the guards before the door were keeping the prison.

*7 Now behold, **an angel of the Lord stood by him,** and a light shone in the prison; and he struck Peter on the side and raised him up, saying, "Arise quickly!" And his chains fell off his hands. 8 Then the angel said to him, "Gird yourself and tie on your sandals;" and so he did. And he said to him, "Put on your garment and follow me."* Acts 12:5-9

But after long abstinence from food, then Paul stood in the midst of them and said, "Men, you should have listened to me, and not have sailed from Crete and incurred this disaster and loss. 22 And now I urge you to take heart, for there will be no loss of life among you, but only of the ship.

*23 For **there stood by me this night an angel of the God** to whom I belong and whom I serve, 24 saying, 'Do not be afraid, Paul; you must be brought before Caesar; and indeed God has granted you all those who sail with you.' 25 Therefore take heart, men, for I believe God that it will be just as it was told me. 26 However, we must run aground on a certain island."* Acts 27:21-26

All these events of visitation and communication occurred after Jesus had resurrected and ascended into heaven. God did nothing different than He did under the Old Covenant relationship. Hebrews, chapter thirteen, verse eight, tells us, Jesus *Christ is the same yesterday and today and forever.* Why is it then that many in the Church believe God no longer talks to His people in this manner? If there is no other truth that you receive from this book, please remember this: God is moved only by faith, and the Bible tells us in Hebrews 11:6:

*But without faith it is impossible to please Him, for he
who comes to God must believe that He is, and that He
is a rewarder of those who diligently seek Him.*

Is it possible that many in the Church today do not hear
from God for the same reason many could not hear Him then?
Can it be that their lack of believing stops the communication
with God?

If we do not believe God will talk to us, is it not a lack of
faith? Why then should God answer those who doubt that He
will talk to them? Peter, Paul, and the other Apostles, believed
and received from God during times of prayer and fasting.
Should we believe or expect anything less?

48

CHAPTER 5

THE HOLY SPIRIT SPEAKS

One of the last teachings Jesus gave his disciples, before His crucifixion, was about the purpose and receiving of the Holy Spirit in the believer's life:

> *"If you love Me, keep My commandments. 16 And I will pray the Father, and He will give you another Helper, that He may abide with you forever — 17 the Spirit of Truth, whom the world cannot receive, because it neither sees Him nor knows Him; but you know Him, for He dwells with you and will be in you. 18 I will not leave you orphans; I will come to you."* John 14:15-18

Jesus told His disciples that He would send a Helper, the Spirit of Truth, which only His Church could receive. The world cannot have relationship with God without the Holy Spirit of God. The word *"abide"* translates from the Greek word *eimi,* and it means; "to exist, live, stay, remain or be in a place" (Thayer's). The assignment of the Holy Spirit is to exist and live with us, and in us. Jesus goes on to define the Holy Spirit's assignment in John 16:5-15:

> *"But now I go away to Him who sent Me, and none of you asks Me, 'Where are You going?' 6 But because I have said these things to you, sorrow has filled your heart. 7 Nevertheless I tell you the truth. It is to your advantage that I go away; for if I do not go away, the Helper will not come to you; but if I depart, I will send*

Him to you. 8 And when He has come, He will convict the world of sin, and of righteousness, and of judgment: 9 of sin, because they do not believe in Me; 10 of righteousness, because I go to My Father and you see Me no more; 11 of judgment, because the ruler of this world is judged.

12 "I still have many things to say to you, but you cannot bear them now. 13 However, when He, the Spirit of truth, has come, He will guide you into all truth; for He will not speak on His own authority, but whatever He hears He will speak; and He will tell you things to come. 14 He will glorify Me, for He will take of what is Mine and declare it to you.

15 All things that the Father has are Mine. Therefore I said that He will take of Mine and declare it to you."

From this passage of Scripture, there should be no misunderstanding as to God's assignment given to the Holy Spirit. This passage of Scripture is the job description of the Holy Spirit. He will guide us in truth. Jesus said in John 14:6, *"I am the truth and the way."* What is the truth? Jesus, the Logos, is the truth of God.

The word *"guide"* is translated from the Greek word *hodeegoo,* which means; "to be a guide, or teacher, to lead on one's way" (Thayer's). It is the mission of the Holy Spirit to lead us on the road of truth. In order for Him to lead us, He will need to give us the discernment to make the right decisions in life. This is how the Logos (word) of God comes alive to us. We will discuss more about this later in this book.

However, this is why we need the Holy Spirit to tell us all things and lead us in truth. How important is the Holy Spirit to all believers? Without Him, we will not come to the truth and understanding of God's word needed for survival in this world. Without Him, we can do nothing. He is the manifested power of God that is to abide in us. This is why it is imperative for every believer in Jesus Christ to pray and, *ask for,* the 'infilling' of the Holy Spirit. This is what Jesus tells us in Luke 11:13:

> *"So I say to you, ask, and it will be given to you; seek, and you will find; knock, and it will be opened to you. 10 For everyone who <u>asks</u> receives, and he who seeks finds, and to him who knocks it will be opened. 11 If a son asks for bread from any father among you, will he give him a stone? Or if he asks for a fish, will he give him a serpent instead of a fish? 12 Or if he asks for an egg, will he offer him a scorpion?*
>
> *13 If you then, being evil, know how to give good gifts to your children,* **how much more will your heavenly Father give the Holy Spirit to those who ask Him!"**

The second most important event in your life will be the day you ask for the infilling of the Holy Spirit. It is second only to the day that you ask Jesus to save your life and accept Him as your Lord and Savior. It is important that we understand that these are two separate events. They take place only when we *ask* for them from God, and we can receive them only by faith.

God is not going to force anyone into a relationship with Himself. He will enter into relationship only with a willing heart. This is the gift of freewill God has given to all of mankind. How many people in your life do you have a relationship with by force? God does not look for forced relationships. Love is a decision we make from a freewill heart, not from fear-based compulsion.

It is only when we ask out of our freewill that God sends His free gift of life, and the Holy Spirit. Without receiving the Holy Spirit, there will be no still small voice speaking to us, guiding us in all things. In fact, one of the Holy Spirit's primary objectives is to speak to us. What is He to say? He is to tell us about things to come, and to declare to us all the things we have obtained in Christ (John 14:26).

Therefore, the question should not be, "Does God talk to His people today" - but rather - "Do God's people have the ears to hear what the Holy Spirit is saying to them?" Have we spent the necessary time with God to discern the voice of His Holy Spirit? Only when we spend the time daily, with Him will we reap the harvest that we sow. If we sow time with God, we will reap time with His presence. Let us not forget that, "*in His presence is fullness of joy.*" With His presence also comes power:

> But **you shall receive power when the Holy Spirit has come upon you**; *and you shall be witnesses to Me in Jerusalem, and in all Judea and Samaria, and to the end of the earth."* Acts 1:8

This is why we should pray, **"Come, Holy Spirit, I want your presence in my life. Speak to me and guide me in all your ways. Lead me in the path of truth, for your word is truth and life to those who find it. Fill me with your power to do your will. Amen!"**

THE INWARD WITNESS – A STILL SMALL VOICE

One of the most intriguing aspects of being a follower of Jesus Christ is to know that He has been resurrected from the dead and is alive today. Not only is Jesus alive, but He wants to talk to His people · today.

There is no other religion in the world that can claim that their god talks to every one of his followers. This is the primary difference between Christianity and other beliefs. Only Christ has been resurrected, and still lives today. All the founders of other religions are dead and talk to no one.

As we discovered, it is a primary responsibility of the Holy Spirit to talk to us, and He tells us only what God the Father and Jesus have to say. Nevertheless, just how does the Holy Spirit talk to us?

One of the most difficult aspects of writing books on the subject of hearing the Holy Spirit is conveying how humans, driven by the human senses (hearing, sight, smell, taste, and touch) can hear and comprehend the spirit world. This was an issue Jesus had even with His disciples.

He remarked repeatedly about someone not having ears to hear. Consequently, it was only after the Holy Spirit came into the disciples' lives that they received the ability to hear what the Holy Spirit had to say. However, is this the only time anyone can hear into the spirit realm? No! People hear into the spirit realm every day...they just do not recognize it when it happens. Since we are a spirit that occupies a body, we all have the ability to hear into the spirit realm with spiritual ears. It is only our lack of discernment, and spiritual training, that prevents us from understanding who is talking, and what is being said and heard. Jesus reveals this truth to the Scribes and Pharisees in John 8:37-47:

> *"I know that you are Abraham's descendants, but you seek to kill Me, because My word has no place in you. 38 I speak what I have seen with My Father, and you do what you have seen with your father." 39 They answered and said to Him, "Abraham is our father." Jesus said to them, "If you were Abraham's children, you would do the works of Abraham. 40 But now you seek to kill Me, a Man who has told you the truth which I heard from God. Abraham did not do this. 41 You do the deeds of your father." Then they said to Him, "We were not born of fornication; we have one Father — God." 42 Jesus said to them, "If God were your Father, you would love Me, for I proceeded forth and came from God; nor have I come of Myself, but He sent Me.*
>
> *43 Why do you not understand My speech? Because you are not able to listen to My word. 44 You are of your father the devil, and the desires of your father you want to do. He was a murderer from the beginning, and does not stand in the truth, because there is no truth in him. When he speaks a lie, he speaks from his own resources, for he is a liar and the father of it.*
>
> *45 But because I tell the truth, you do not believe Me. 46 Which of you convicts Me of sin? And if I tell the truth, why do you not believe Me? 47 **He who is of God hears God's words;** therefore you do not hear, because you are not of God."*

Jesus tells them that they cannot hear what God is saying, but they do hear what the devil is saying, and that they seek to do his will, (that is to kill a man). They cannot hear the word of God, because they have not had their spirits renewed to life with God (they were not born again). However, Jesus said their human spirit does hear from the spiritual realm. To whom is the devil talking to when he speaks (verse 44)?

The spirit of man is the gateway into the spirit realm. It is through this gateway that mankind hears with spiritual ears. **The questions are, "What are we listening to" and "How do we recognize our own thoughts from those of spiritual influence?"**

It is through the ears of the human spirit that thoughts are planted into our minds. This explains why Apostle Paul tells us to, "*Bring every thought into captivity to the obedience of Christ*" (2 Cor. 10:5). It is only through our own arrogance, or lack of knowledge, that we believe that every thought we have is our own. Only by taking control of our thought life can we experience the victorious life God intends for us to live.

This brings us to the importance of reading and meditating, the Word of God. Jesus said, "***The words*** *that I speak to you* ***are spirit***, *and they* ***are life***" (John 6:63-64). This is a very important statement, because it tells us that what Jesus is saying is spirit inspired, and explains why only a few could hear and comprehend what He said. Only those with spiritual ears to hear understood. Most importantly, it is with these words that we are to feed our mind and spirit, for they produce life, and they will speak to us in time of need.

The Holy Spirit will speak these words to us in difficult times...when you need to hear from God. The Holy Spirit will tell us nothing that contradicts God's word. **He will speak to us in a calm voice, because there is no fear, panic, or distress in the voice of the Holy Spirit of God.**

Most often, we interpret His voice as intuition, or something that seems right in our heart. Sometimes we associate what we hear from the Holy Spirit as our conscience speaking to us.

Whatever you want to call His voice, it will be a still calm voice that you hear from within your heart...the home of your human spirit. Regardless of your situation, God will speak to you. If you will spend the time with Him, you will train yourself to hear with your spiritual ears just what the Spirit of God is saying to you. **Does God talk to His people today? Yes! Do we have ears trained to hear?**

> *"Behold, I send you out as sheep in the midst of wolves. Therefore be wise as serpents and harmless as doves. 17 But beware of men, for they will deliver you up to councils and scourge you in their synagogues.*
>
> *18 You will be brought before governors and kings for My sake, as a testimony to them and to the Gentiles. 19 But when they deliver you up, do not worry about how or what you should speak. For it will be given to you in that hour what you should speak; 20 **for it is not you who speak, but the Spirit of your Father who speaks in you.**"* Matt. 10:16-20

CHAPTER 6

FRUIT PRODUCERS

"Ho! Everyone who thirsts, come to the waters; And you who have no money, come, buy and eat. Yes, come, buy wine and milk without money and without price. 2 Why do you spend money for what is not bread, and your wages for what does not satisfy? Listen carefully to Me, and eat what is good, and let your soul delight itself in abundance.

3 Incline your ear, and come to Me. Hear, and your soul shall <u>live</u>; And I will make an everlasting covenant with you — *The sure mercies of David. 4 Indeed I have given him as a witness to the people a leader and commander for the people. 5 Surely you shall call a nation you do not know, And nations who do not know you shall run to you, because of the LORD your God, And the Holy One of Israel; For He has glorified you."*

6 Seek the LORD while He may be found, call upon Him while He is near. 7 Let the wicked forsake his way, And the unrighteous man his thoughts; Let him return to the LORD, And He will have mercy on him; And to our God, For He will abundantly pardon. 8 "For My thoughts are not your thoughts, nor are your ways My ways," says the LORD. 9 "For as the heavens are higher than the earth, so are My ways higher than your ways, And My thoughts than your thoughts.

10 "For as the rain comes down, and the snow from heaven, and do not return there, but water the earth, and make it bring forth and bud, that it may give seed to the sower and bread to the eater, 11 so shall My word be that goes forth from My mouth; It shall not return to Me void, But it shall accomplish what I please, and it shall prosper in the thing for which I sent it. 12 "For you shall go out with joy, and be led out with peace; The mountains and the hills shall break forth into singing before you, and all the trees of the field shall clap their hands. 13 Instead of the thorn shall come up the cypress tree, and instead of the brier shall come up the myrtle tree; And it shall be to the LORD for a name, for an everlasting sign that shall not be cut off." Isaiah 55:1-13

The first thing God talks about in this passage is the depraved state of being, in which man lives. We have a thirst for what money cannot buy, and what the world cannot supply. **It is only through relationship with God that the soul of man can be satisfied.** We think we have abundance, yet we lack what the world cannot offer; the abundance that is available only through God. He said if we will incline our ear and come to Him, our souls shall **live**, and He will make covenant with us.

The Hebrew word for "*live*", used in this passage is *chayah,* and it means, "to have life, remain alive, **sustain life**, **live prosperously**, **live forever**, be quickened, be alive, **be restored to life or health**" (Brown Driver & Briggs Hebrew Lexicon). It can be used in the sense of restoring something back to its original condition. We can be restored back to our original relationship to God, before the fall of Adam and Eve - a place where God supplied man's every need, and most importantly, where Adam walked and talked with God:

> And **they heard the sound of the LORD God walking in the garden in the cool of the day**, and Adam and his wife hid themselves from the presence of the LORD God among the trees of the garden. 9 Then the LORD God called to Adam and said to him, "Where are you?" 10 So he said, "**I heard Your voice** in the garden, and I was afraid because I was naked; and I hid myself." Gen. 3:8-10

Adam and Eve heard the voice of God, and recognized His voice. This means they must have heard His voice many times before, but sin would change the relationship. Sin would separate man from the righteous and holy God. However, God wants that relationship with man restored. This begs the question: How is it possible? How can a sinful man be made righteous again? God reveals the answer to this question starting in Isaiah fifty-five verse ten. It will be by the power of His word. He said that His word shall not return void. What word is going to restore man's relationship with God? We see the answer in John 1:1-5:

> **In the beginning was the Word, and the Word was with God, and the Word was God**. 2 He was in the beginning with God. 3 All things were made through Him, and without Him nothing was made that was made. 4 In Him was life, and the life was the light of men. 5 And the light shines in the darkness, and the darkness did not comprehend it.

John goes on to write in verse 14,

And the Word became flesh and dwelt among us, and we beheld His glory, the glory as of the only begotten of the Father, full of grace and truth.

The word John is writing about is the *Word* of God manifest in his Son, Jesus Christ. Jesus was the *Word* of God made flesh. Born as a man, Jesus Christ, the Son of God, came to Earth to redeem man from the curse of sin...paying the price for man's sin. He did everything required to restore man's relationship to God.

In the beginning was the *word.* The Greek word translated as, *word,* in this passage is, *Logos.* We will examine the importance and difference of this Greek word, *Logos,* as compared to a second Greek word, *Rhema,* that is also translated as *word* in the English language in the following chapters. It is only when we understand the different meanings of these two words, *Logos* and *Rhema, that* we obtain the full impact of the message God is giving to His people. Furthermore, it is only through this understanding that we will live the victorious life God has intended for us to live.

CHAPTER 7

THE LOGOS

What does the Greek word "*Logos*" mean? Let us examine several definitions from some of the leading translations and commentaries.

Logos - a word spoken for any purpose (Vine's Expository Dictionary of Biblical Words).

Logos - logos, logou, - a collecting or collection: As in respect to speech: a word which, uttered by the living voice, **embodies a conception or idea**; what someone has said; a saying; discourse; the act of speaking, speech: reason, the mental faculty of thinking, meditating, **reasoning**, calculating, account, **consideration, reckoning**, score (Thayer's Greek Lexicon).

Logos — (log'-os); **something said (including the thought)**; by implication a topic **(subject of discourse)**, also **reasoning** (the mental faculty) or motive; by extension, a computation; specifically (with the article in John) the Divine Expression (New Exhaustive Strong's Numbers and Concordance with Expanded Greek-Hebrew Dictionary).

If we were to condense or consolidate these translations, a good definition would be "**reasoned thought, expressed through speech or writing; to speak or write what's on one's mind**. It has been said, that men sometimes engage their mouths before they engage their brains. This saying implies that we often say things *before* we think about what we are saying. This **would not** be Logos. Logos implies that we express or articulate something that we have put thought into before it proceeds from our mouths, or is written.

This definition of the word "Logos" gives us a better understanding of what John was expressing when he wrote:

> *In the beginning was* **the Word, and the Word was with God, and the Word was God.** *2 He was in the beginning with God. 3 All things were made through Him, and without Him nothing was made that was made. 4 In Him was life, and the life was the light of men. 5 And the light shines in the darkness, and the darkness did not comprehend it.* John 1:1-5

As we now know this word "Logos" was Jesus Christ, sent to this world to fulfill God's plan for man's salvation.

> *And* **the Word (Logos) became flesh and dwelt among us, and we beheld His glory,** *the glory as of the only begotten of the Father, full of grace and truth.* John 1:14

This tells us that God's plan for man's salvation was not an emergency plan, or some impulsive reaction to man's sin, but a well thought out and conceived plan from the beginning of creation. This also reveals to us the thought God put into the Scriptures as they are written to us:

> *All* **Scripture is given by inspiration of God,** *and is profitable for doctrine, for reproof, for correction, for instruction in righteousness, 17 that the man of God may be complete, thoroughly equipped for every good work.* 2 Tim. 3:16-17

A great picture of Logos is given when Jesus compared it to a seed.

Mark 4:3-9

> *"Listen to this! Behold, **the sower went out to sow;** 4 as he was sowing, some seed fell beside the road, and the birds came and ate it up. 5 "Other **seed fell** on the rocky ground where it did not have much soil; and immediately it sprang up because it had no depth of soil. 6 "And after the sun had risen, it was scorched; and because it had no root, it withered away. 7 "**Other seed** fell among the thorns, and the thorns came up and choked it, and it yielded no crop. 8 "**Other seeds** fell into the good soil, and as they grew up and increased, they yielded a crop and produced thirty, sixty, and a hundredfold." 9 And He was saying, "He who has ears to hear, let him hear."*

Why is this of significance to us? First, it tells us the Logos is compared to seed. Jesus goes on to explain this in Mark 4:13-15:

> *And He said to them, "Do you not understand this parable? How will you understand all the parables? 14 "**The sower sows the word (Logos)"**.*

Secondly, we get a great understanding of the Word (Logos) as seed in Numbers 11:7-9:

> *Now the manna **was like coriander seed**, and its appearance like that of bdellium. 8 The people would go about and gather it and grind it between two millstones or beat it in the mortar, and boil it in the pot and make cakes with it; and its taste was as the taste of cakes baked with*

63

oil. 9 When the dew fell on the camp at night, the manna would fall with it.

God provided two things in the wilderness. Manna was a seed that was used to make cakes for food. Israel was to live on the Logos that God rained down to them — a seed that is to be planted in them. Secondly, He provided water. We will discuss what the symbolism of water is in chapter twelve.

The bible that we read is the Logos (Manna, Word) of God, and it is His reasoned and articulated thoughts to us. Some people will argue that the Bible is just a book put together by men. However, this is just a misunderstanding of what the Bible really represents.

The Bible is a miracle unto itself. The Bible, as we know it, is a book composed of sixty-six letters. The exact number of writers we do not know. However, we do know that many men who never knew each other personally wrote it over thousands of years. Yet, its common theme is woven throughout the entire book by only one author - God.

The word *"Scripture"* means, Holy writings, and inspiration; which connotes that they are divinely breathed.

The Apostle Paul's letter to Timothy tells us that what he and the other writers of the Bible are expressing are the thoughts of God revealed to men, by the Holy Spirit, for man to live by. It becomes important for us to understand that these are not just words, but that these words (Logos) produce fruit in our lives as God looks over His words (Logos) to perform it, or make it come to pass. These fruits are what make the Logos so significant to our lives. This brings us to the point of verse seventeen, *"that the man of God may be complete"*.

This begs the question, "what are these fruits"? Logos, the written word of God, produces three fruits in the believer's life. We will call these three fruits, **our defensive armaments**. These truths will become apparent as we discuss the function of each fruit.

CHAPTER 8

THE FRUITS OF LOGOS

As we recall the parable of the sower in Luke chapter four, Jesus tells us that, "*The sower sows the word*". The Greek word used in this passage is Logos (word). Jesus tells us that there is a reaping of thirty, sixty, or one hundred-fold, so it becomes obvious that there are fruits produced from the seed sown. What is the fruit produced?

SPIRITUAL WISDOM

The first fruit that Logos produces is **wisdom.** Wisdom starts with a reverence for God. The Scripture tells us in Proverbs 9:10,

"The fear of the LORD is the beginning of wisdom, And the knowledge of the Holy One is understanding."

This does not mean a fear of God in the sense of being afraid of Him, but rather a reverence for God. We should give all our respect to our Heavenly Father, our creator and loving God.

What is the *wisdom* that Logos produces? James 3:13-8 gives us an answer to this question:

Who is wise and understanding among you? Let him show by good conduct that his works are done in the meekness of wisdom. 14 But if you have bitzer envy and

self-seeking in your hearts, do not boast and lie against the truth. 15 This wisdom does not descend from above, but is earthly, sensual, and demonic.

16 For where envy and self-seeking exist, confusion and every evil thing are there. 17 But the wisdom that is from above is first pure, then peaceable, gentle, willing to yield, full of mercy and good fruits, without partiality and without hypocrisy. 18 Now the fruit of righteousness is sown in peace by those who make peace.

Proverbs two, verse six, tells us that, *"the LORD gives wisdom; From His mouth come knowledge and understanding."*

We read here that there are two types of wisdom: **earthly (carnal)** and **heavenly (spiritual)**. James is telling us that there is a worldly wisdom that produces a self-seeking fruit which is driven by selfish desire, and lust for the world. However, there is also a spiritual wisdom that produces a different fruit for our lives. We read about the fruit that spiritual wisdom produces in Proverbs 2:1-9, as Solomon wrote:

*My son, if you receive my words, and treasure my commands within you, 2 So that you incline your ear to wisdom, and apply your heart to understanding; 3 Yes, if you cry out for discernment, And lift up your voice for **understanding**, 4 If you seek her as silver, and search for her as for hidden treasures; 5 Then you will understand the fear of the LORD, and find the knowledge of God.*

*6 For **the LORD gives wisdom; From His mouth come knowledge and understanding;** 7 He stores up **sound wisdom** for the upright; He is a shield to those who walk uprightly; 8 He guards the paths of justice, and preserves the way of His saints. 9 Then you will understand righteousness and justice, equity and every good path.*

What is the value of these fruits for you? We find a good response to this question in Proverbs 8:12-22,

*"I, wisdom, dwell with prudence, and I find **knowledge** and **discretion**. 13 The fear of the LORD is to hate evil; Pride and arrogance and the evil way and the perverted mouth, I hate. 14 Counsel is mine and sound wisdom; I am understanding, power is mine.*

15 By me kings reign, and rulers decree justice. 16 By me princes rule, and nobles, all who judge rightly. 17 I love those who love me; and those who diligently seek me will find me. 18 Riches and honor are with me, enduring wealth and righteousness. 19 My fruit is better than gold, even pure gold, and my yield better than choicest silver. 20 I walk in the way of righteousness, in the midst of the paths of justice, 21 to endow those who love me with wealth, that I may fill their treasuries." NASU

There are people that believe all Christians should live lives of poverty, yet the very essence of receiving God's Logos is to obtain wisdom, understanding, discretion, sound counsel, and prudence; the results of which will lead us to having a direct relationship with God. Moreover, in His presence we can find fullness of joy, peace, health, wealth, and filled treasuries:

How blessed is the man who finds wisdom and the man who gains understanding. 14 For her profit is better than the profit of silver and her gain better than fine gold. 15 She is more precious than jewels; And nothing you desire compares with her. 16 Long life is in her right hand; In her left hand are riches and honor.

17 Her ways are pleasant ways and all her paths are peace. 18 She is a tree of life to those who take hold of her, and happy are all who hold her fast. Proverbs 3:13-18 NASU

A man named Solomon was the principal writer God used for the book of Proverbs. Who was Solomon, and what did he ask of God? <u>Solomon was one of the sons of Israel's king David.</u> When Solomon became king, he asked for one thing from God:

Therefore, give to Your servant an understanding heart to judge Your people, that I may discern between good and evil. For who is able to judge this great people of Yours?" 1 Kings 3:8-9

Solomon then became the wisest king to ever rule over Israel, and the richest man in history.

And God gave Solomon wisdom and exceedingly great understanding, and largeness of heart like the sand on the seashore. 1 Kings 4:29

So what is spiritual wisdom? Spiritual wisdom is having insight into the true nature of things. Spiritual wisdom goes beyond earthly wisdom, in that it reveals or brings to light the hidden agendas of a corrupt world system. Its foundation is truth, and it is not altered by circumstances or facts that are subject to change. This is because **truth never changes**. The more you read God's Logos, the more He will reveal to you His good intentions for your life and the spiritual wisdom God has for you. This type of wisdom can be obtained only through fellowship with God and His Logos, Jesus Christ, the Logos made flesh.

What is this other type of wisdom called, 'carnal wisdom'? Carnal wisdom is the worldly wisdom obtained through the five senses of the flesh. Let me first preface by saying that there is some good worldly wisdom. For example, we learn that a hot stove will burn us if we touch it. We gain wisdom from that type of experience and from those who share that wisdom.

Since the fall of Adam, the seed of sin has corrupted man's flesh and reasoning, distorting what may be truth. This is why the Apostle Paul tells us that the Christian should; *"walk by faith not by sight"* (2Cor. 5:7). What we see, and then reason, may be in direct opposition to what the word of God tells us.

This will bring us to another point of decision. Do we believe what we see, or believe what God's word says about our situation? Corrupted carnal thinking will not lead us to faith in God and His word. It will not lead us to the point of God moving on our behalf; because, *"without faith it is impossible to please Him"* (Heb. 11:6).

SPIRITUAL DISCERNMENT

A second fruit that comes through Logos, and is closely associated to wisdom, is *spiritual discernment.* Discernment is an extremely important **defensive armament** for our survival.

71

*Let us therefore be diligent to enter that rest, lest anyone fall according to the same example of disobedience. 12 For **the word (Logos) of God is living and powerful,** and sharper than any two-edged sword, piercing even to the division of soul and spirit, and of joints and marrow, and **is a discerner** of the thoughts and intents of the heart. 13 And there is no creature hidden from His sight, but all things are naked and open to the eyes of Him to whom we must give account.* Heb. 4:11-13

It is important to take note that this passage declares the Logos to be a discerner. It is living and powerful and *nothing is hidden* from His sight. His sight is a reference to Jesus Christ, the Logos made flesh and the Son of God. This armament of discernment is so important for every Christian that the Apostle Paul explains its use in 2 Corinthians 10:4-5;

*For the armaments of our warfare are not carnal but mighty in God for pulling down strongholds, 5 casting down arguments and every high thing that exalts itself against the knowledge of God, **bringing every thought into captivity to the obedience of Christ.***

We are to bring every thought into captivity to the obedience of Christ (the Logos). What does that mean? **Discernment reveals and separates truth from lies**. We have an enemy who has set his heart on our destruction. Just as he tempted Jesus in the wilderness, he tempts everyone today:

Then Jesus, being filled with the Holy Spirit, returned from the Jordan and was led by the Spirit into the wilderness, 2 being tempted for forty days by the devil.

And in those days He ate nothing, and afterward, when they had ended, He was hungry.

*3 And the devil said to Him, "**If You are the Son of God**, command this stone to become bread." 4 But Jesus answered him, saying, "It is written, 'Man shall not live by bread alone, but by every word of God.'"*

5 Then the devil, taking Him up on a high mountain, showed Him all the kingdoms of the world in a moment of time. 6 And the devil said to Him, "All this authority I will give You, and their glory; for this has been delivered to me, and I give it to whomever I wish. 7 Therefore, if You will worship before me, all will be Yours."

*8 And Jesus answered and said to him, "Get behind Me, Satan! For it is written, 'You shall worship the LORD your God, and Him only you shall serve.'" 9 Then he brought Him to Jerusalem, set Him on the pinnacle of the temple, and said to Him, "**If You are the Son of God**, throw Yourself down from here. 10 For it is written: 'He shall give His angels charge over you, to keep you,' 11 and, 'In their hands they shall bear you up, lest you dash your foot against a stone.'"*

12 And Jesus answered and said to him, "It has been said, 'You shall not tempt the LORD your God.'" 13 Now when the devil had ended every temptation, he departed from Him until an opportune time. Luke 4:1-13

Just as the devil took scripture out of context to try to deceive Jesus, he will do the same to us. We have noted that Jesus is the Logos of God. Jesus discerned or compared the scripture the devil quoted to Himself, the Logos, the expressed reasoned thoughts of God. He then cast down the misrepresented or twisted Logos the devil was using to try to kill Him.

If we do not have the Logos abiding in us to provide discernment, we become easy targets for his deception and destruction. This is because our enemy, Satan, works primarily in our thought life, making our soul the battleground for spiritual warfare. This is why Paul tells us to *take every thought captive"*.

If we cannot discern the truth from the lie, we will live a defeated life, or even worse, die in defeat. If we do not have discernment, we will not know who is talking to us, be it God or the devil. Without Logos we will be deceived.

One of the great deceptions of all time is seen when Christians become sick and then believe that God has put sickness upon them to teach them something. Nothing could be further from the truth, yet many Christians believe this lie. If God were to put sickness upon His own children, He would be nullifying the very works that Jesus suffered and died on the cross to obtain for His Church. We find this truth in 1 Peter 2:24,

> *Who Himself bore our sins in His own body on the tree, that we, having died to sins, might live for righteousness — by whose stripes you were healed.*

This is a confirmation of what the prophet Isaiah prophesied in Isaiah 53:1-6:

Who has believed our report? And to whom has the arm of the LORD been revealed? 2 For He shall grow up before Him as a tender plant, and as a root out of dry ground. He has no form or comeliness; And when we see Him, there is no beauty that we should desire Him.

3 He is despised and rejected by men, A Man of sorrows and acquainted with **grief**. *And we hid, as it were, our faces from Him; He was despised, and we did not esteem Him. 4 Surely He has borne our* **griefs** *and carried our sorrows; Yet we esteemed Him stricken, smitten by God, and afflicted. 5 But He was wounded for our transgressions, He was bruised for our iniquities; The chastisement for our peace was upon Him, and by His stripes we are healed.*

6 All we like sheep have gone astray; We have turned, every one, to his own way; And the LORD has laid on Him the iniquity of us all. NKJV

The English word "*grief*" translates from the Hebrew word *choliy* (khol-ee'), which is most often defined as, "disease or sickness" (Englishman's Concordance). A good example of this is in the King James translation of Deuteronomy 7:15:

And the LORD will take away from thee all **_sickness_** (*choliy* (khol-ee'), *and will put none of the evil diseases of Egypt, which thou knowest, upon thee; but will lay them upon all them that hate thee.*

Sickness and disease are the byproduct of the curse of the Law. The curse and its results are the very reason Jesus came to redeem mankind:

> *Christ has redeemed us from the curse of the law,* *having become a curse for us (for it is written, "Cursed is everyone who hangs on a tree"), 14 that the blessing of Abraham might come upon the Gentiles in Christ Jesus, that we might receive the promise of the Spirit through faith.* Gal. 3:13-14

Here we find an absolute truth established throughout eternity in that there is no way under heaven that God would set aside what His Son, Jesus, suffered and died for on the cross.

SPIRITUAL KNOWLEDGE

The third fruit that works closely with wisdom and discernment is **knowledge.** There are **two types of knowledge - *carnal and spiritual.***

"*Carnal knowledge*", relates closely to the Hebrew word, *yada`*, a verb, and it essentially means; "to know by experiencing" or "knowledge gained through the senses." This verb can also mean, "to be acquainted with," a kind of intellectual awareness (Vine's). It may be used in gaining knowledge from books we read or news we hear. It would be used in the instance of a wife and husband having an intimate experiential knowledge of each other.

Some carnal knowledge may be bad. For example, we have all seen good worldly knowledge save lives through medical treatments and safety procedures. However, worldly knowledge can be distorted, or inaccurate, because it is communicated and obtained through a corrupted flesh and reasoning process. Carnal knowledge may result in pride. We sometimes see this in the business world, with successful people, or the medical field when **some physicians**, **not all**, have more faith in their knowledge and ability, than faith in God's ability.

On the other hand, *spiritual knowledge* would be more related to the Hebrew word, *"da`ath"*, which means; "to know about, be aware of, or taught by God" (Brown-Drive-Briggs). The word *"da'ath"*, used in Proverbs 2:6 connotes knowing about God:

For the LORD gives wisdom; From His mouth come knowledge (da'ath) and understanding;

Psalm 94:10, continues to tell us man can be taught, *da'ath* (knowledge) by God:

He who instructs the nations, shall He not correct, He who teaches man knowledge?

This type of spiritual knowledge will lead us into a deeper relationship with God, but it comes only from the Holy Spirit giving us insight into the spiritual realm, and the world system. God gives us spiritual ears to hear His Logos (word).

It is essential for victorious Christian living, that we obtain this spiritual insight as to how the world system thinks and operates. Solomon gives us a great example of worldly thinking in Proverbs 7:6-14:

*For at the window of my house I looked through my lattice, 7 and saw among the simple, I perceived among the youths, a young man **devoid of understanding**, 8 passing along the street near her corner; And he took the path to her house 9 in the twilight, in the evening, in the black and dark night.*

10 And there a woman met him, with the attire of a harlot, and a crafty heart. 11 she was loud and rebellious, her feet would not stay at home. 12 At times she was outside, at times in the open square, lurking at every corner. 13 So she caught him and kissed him; With an impudent face she said to him: 14 "I have peace offerings with me;

Drop to vs 21 -23

*With her enticing speech she caused him to yield, with her flattering lips she seduced him. 22 Immediately he went after her, as an ox goes to the slaughter, or as a fool to the correction of the stocks, 23 till an arrow struck his liver. As a bird hastens to the snare, **he did not know it would cost his life.***

The passage not only speaks of the fleshly trap, but spiritually speaking, the "she" that Solomon writes about in this proverb may represent the world system, and the young man devoid of understanding is a man with no Word of God working in his life.

It is Logos that teaches us the truth about the corruption of the world system, how it works, and the end result...if we choose to live by its standards. Logos provides the spiritual discernment needed for us to prevent many of the tribulations of life that we encounter. If we will plant the Logos of God in our hearts, it will produce the spiritual fruits of wisdom, discernment, and knowledge. The end-result will be a life of prosperity and victory. God says He looks over His word (Logos) to perform it, and it (His Word) shall not return to Him void (Isa. 55:11). **God guarantees its results!**

UNDERSTANDING

The fourth fruit of Logos is, ***understanding.*** The word, *"understanding",* is translated from the Hebrew word *biyn* (bene), which is a primitive Hebrew root word meaning; "to separate mentally or distinguish, (generally) understand, perceive, or have intelligence about something" (Strong's).

How does understanding differ from wisdom? The difference is quite simple. It is one thing to understand how something operates, however; it is another to have the wisdom to know when to use it. Some great examples of this may be read in what Solomon wrote in Ecclesiastes 3:1-8:

> *To everything there is a season, A time for every purpose under heaven:2 A time to be born, And a time to die; A time to plant, And a time to pluck what is planted; 3 A time to kill, And a time to heal; A time to break down, And a time to build up; 4 A time to weep, And a time to laugh; A time to mourn, And a time to dance; 5 A time to cast away stones, And a time to gather stones; A time to embrace, And a time to refrain from embracing; 6 A time to gain, And a time to lose; A time to keep, And a time to throw away; 7 A time to tear, And a time to sew; A time to keep silence, And a*

time to speak; 8 A time to love, And a time to hate; A time of war, And a time of peace.

Many of Solomon's points pertain to having the wisdom of timing and knowledge, and the understanding of what to do with them.

A farmer needs the wisdom of knowing when to plant. If he plants in the beginning of winter, he is just wasting his time and money. If he plants in a field that is too wet, his crop may not survive. He may have all the knowledge and understanding of how seeds work and how to plant, but wisdom of timing can be the difference between harvest and no harvest.

We find great examples of how the Holy Spirit directed the Apostle Paul as to timing in the Book of Acts.

Acts 16:6-9

*They passed through the Phrygian and Galatian region, **having been forbidden by the Holy Spirit to speak the word in Asia**; 7 and after they came to Mysia, they were trying to go into Bithynia, and **the Spirit of Jesus did not permit them;** 8 and passing by Mysia, they came down to Troas.*

Acts 19:9-10

*But when some were becoming hardened and disobedient, speaking evil of the Way before the people, he withdrew from them and took away the disciples, reasoning daily in the school of Tyrannus. 10 This took place for two years, **so that all who lived in Asia heard the word of the Lord**, both Jews and Greeks.*

CHAPTER 9

RHEMA

The second Greek word, "*Rhema*" that we want to examine is also translated into the English as, "*word*". However, its meaning is completely different, and its usage is of the utmost importance to every believer. Just as Logos produces fruit, Rhema also produces fruit, but a different kind of fruit.

Producing fruit should be of no surprise to anyone who reads the Bible. We understand that from the very beginning of creation, God gave Adam a command: *Be fruitful and multiply* (Gen. 1:28). As I stated previously, God created us to be fruit producers, so the question is not if we produce fruit, but what kind of fruit do we produce...good or bad? This prompts a second question: How do we produce this fruit?

We are made in God's image, (Gen. 1:27) and therefore, we will produce fruit by what proceeds from our mouth and what we do with our hands...just as God produced fruit by the words of His mouth and shaped man with the work of His hands.

This is where Rhema becomes important for us to understand, not only how it is different in meaning from Logos, but also how its function is different from Logos. As mentioned previously, *Logos* is defined as "reasoned speech or articulated thought put forth in speech or writings." *Rhema* however, is defined by Thayer's as "that which is or has been uttered by the living voice, a thing spoken, a word; any sound produced by the voice and having a definite meaning." However, I like to relate the word more closely to the Apostle Paul's definition in Ephesians 6:17:

> And take the helmet of salvation, and **the sword of the Spirit, which is the word (rhema) of God;**

At the time of Paul's writing to the Ephesian Church, he was confined to the prison at the Roman garrison in Rome. Paul would have seen many Roman soldiers and their armament during his confinement there. The Greek word for, "*sword*", that Paul uses to compare the *Rhema* of God to, comes from the Greek word *machaira* (makh'-ahee-rah), and it defines it as a "short sword or knife." This gives the idea of comparing Rhema, as Paul did, to the primary armament that the Roman soldier commonly carried on his side into battle. It was an armament used for tight hand-to-hand combat.

If we are to rightly believe that the Apostle Paul's writings are inspired by the Holy Spirit, it would stand to reason that Paul, inspired by God, used the right word, *Rhema*, rather than, *Logos,* for this passage of scripture to make a point.

Rhema, is *"the sword of the Spirit"*, making it spirit-inspired word. This type of sword was used in battle primarily as an **offensive armament,** just as *Rhema* is to be used as an offensive armament against our enemy in spiritual battle. God has fully equipped His saints with the armaments needed to live victoriously in this life, both for defensive (*Logos*), and for offensive (*Rhema*) warfare. The question is: What do we do with this armor and armaments?

Please note, it is not my intent to confuse you with too many Greek definitions, so please bear with me as we study the next passage of scripture in **Ephesians 6:10-19.** It is important to our understanding of what the Apostle Paul is telling us to do. He is going to give us two distinctive actions we must take for our survival in this fallen world:

*Finally, my brethren, be strong in the Lord and in the power of His might. 11 **Put on** the whole armor of God, that you may be able to stand against the wiles of the devil. 12 For we do not wrestle against flesh and blood, but against principalities, against powers, against the rulers of the darkness of this age, against spiritual hosts of wickedness in the heavenly places.*

*13 Therefore **take up** the whole armor of God, that you may be able to withstand in the evil day, and **having** done all, to stand. 14 Stand therefore, **having** girded your waist with truth, **having put on** the breastplate of righteousness, 15 and **having** shod your feet with the preparation of the gospel of peace; 16 above all, **taking** the shield of faith with which you will be able to quench all the fiery darts of the wicked one.*

*17 And **take** the helmet of salvation, and the sword of the Spirit, which is the **word** (Rhema) of God; 18 praying always with all prayer and supplication in the Spirit, being watchful to this end with all perseverance and supplication for all the saints.*

Paul instructs us to do two things: "**Put on**" and "**take up**" the armor. The armor that we **put on** is **our defensive armaments:** The girding of our waist with the truth; the breastplate of righteousness; the helmet of Salvation; and our feet shod with the Gospel are obtained by the Logos of Christ. The shield of faith, the sword of the Spirit, (which is the *Rhema* of God), and the prayers in the Spirit are all *Rhema* inspired **offensive armaments.**

We must note, that the distinction is made by what we **put on** as compared to what we **take up.** Although the word **take** is added in verse seventeen, it is not in the original Greek and was added by the translators. However, in 1 Thessalonians 5:8, Paul tells us to *"**put on** as a helmet, the hope of salvation"*.

The question may come to mind as to how a shield is used offensively. The shield was used in two ways. One way was to shield the soldier from the blows inflicted by the enemy (defensively); however, it was also used to push back an attacking opponent to gain ground (offensively). In addition, shields would be locked together to establish a solid wall to both repel an attack, and to push back attackers. The helmet was used to protect the head from blows (defensively). It is important to note, it is called the helmet of salvation.

Having the Rhema of our salvation not only protects our soul, but also establishes our attitude against the enemy.

What is "salvation"? **Salvation is defined as our deliverance, healing, prosperity, safety, and preservation.**

Salvation comes from the Greek word *soteria*, a noun, which means it is something we take hold of or obtain. When we have it, it will also establish our attitude of aggression against the enemy who wants to steal it from us. If we do not know who we are in Christ, our established salvation, we are bound for defeat. Knowing our salvation protects our mind from the mind games the enemy wants to use against us.

"Put on", is translated from the Greek word *enduo* (en-doo'-o), and it is used in the sense of sinking into a garment; to invest with clothing (literally or figuratively), array with clothes, or to have (put) on (Strong's). Furthermore, *enduo,* is comprised of two Greek root words. The first word is, *en* (en), a primary preposition denoting a (fixed) position in place, time, state and (by implication) instrumentality (medially or constructively); i.e. **a position of rest** (Strong's). In addition, it is also used for that with which a person is **surrounded, equipped**, and **furnished** (Thayer's).

The second Greek root word is, *dunoo,* which means; "to go into or enter, **be plunged into**, or sink into" (Thayer's). If we apply these meanings to the Logos of God, Jesus Christ the word made flesh: **we are to plunge ourselves into a place of rest, totally enveloped in Jesus and God's word.** It is important to note that the word **having** (verse 13) denotes a past-tense action.

We cannot **take up** other parts of the armor, the offensive armaments, until we have **put on** the defensive armaments obtained through the *Logos* and entering that place of rest in Christ. **If we do not put our total faith and confidence in Him, (the Logos, our defense), we are defenseless.**

"Take up", comes from the Greek word *analambano* (an-al-am-ban'-o), and it means, "to take up or receive up" (Strong's). This word, *analambano,* is also composed of two Greek root words. The first is, *ana"* (an-ah'), a primary preposition and adverb, properly meaning "**up**."

The second Greek word is *lambano* (lam-ban'-o), a prolonged form of a primary verb, which is used only as an alternate in certain tenses; "to take, **get hold of in a sense of** seizing with the hand, take hold of what is offered to one for one's personal use" (Strong's). Thayer's defines it this way, "to take with the hand, lay hold of, take in order to carry away, make one's own, lay hold upon, take possession of, or take a thing due according to an agreement or law."

The word "taking", used in verse sixteen is yet another Greek word *dechomai* (dekh'-om-ahee), which signifies "to accept," by a deliberate and ready reception of what is offered (Vine's). It is almost synonymous with *lambano,* but is distinct from it in that *lambano,* sometimes means "to receive as merely a self-prompted action"; without necessarily signifying a favorable reception (Vine's). The distinction is recognized by the attitude of the heart when one takes hold of the armament.

Receive (dechomai) with gladness the engrafted word (Logos), which is able to save your soul, James 1:21.

It is important to remember that we can also *lambano,* take hold of things we do not want, such as a bad doctor's report. This is why we should be cautious of what we see and hear. It is possible for us to be in a battle with only part of the armor on, at which time we will discover that we are fighting a spiritual battle with a distinct disadvantage.

A book that I encourage everyone to read titled, *Dressed to Kill,* by Dr. Rick Renner, gives in-depth detail and understanding of the full armor that God has supplied to His Church.

I understand there are some Bible teachers who believe there is no difference between Logos and Rhema. However, in so doing, they fail to answer the question as to why the words are used in different situations in the Bible. They rightly claim that the entire Bible is the inspired word of God. This truth is confirmed in 2 Timothy 3:16:

All Scripture is given by inspiration of God, and is profitable for doctrine, for reproof, for correction, for instruction in righteousness, 17 that the man of God may be complete, thoroughly equipped for every good work.

The very words, *inspiration of God,* literally means, "to be inspired or breathed of God" (Vine's). The question is not which one is most important, Rhema or Logos, but how each brings a benefit to the Church.

Those who want to deny that God speaks to His Church today are no different that the Scribes and Pharisees that Jesus had to deal with 2000 years ago. They had no ears to hear then, and many have no ears to hear today. Many who criticize Christians claiming to hear the voice of God today, do so because they have never heard the voice of God themselves. It was Jesus who said, **"My sheep hear my voice."** He also said that He would send the Holy Spirit to lead and speak to us:

*"However, when He, **the Spirit of truth** has come, He will guide you into all truth; for He will not speak on His own authority, but **whatever He hears He will speak; and He will tell you things to come.** "* John 16:13-14

To deny this truth, is to deny part of the very mission of the Holy Spirit.

Several years ago, as I was driving down I-71 during rush hour traffic, I distinctly heard the voice of the Holy Spirit tell be to slow down because a vehicle in the right lane was going to cut me off. No sooner than I applied my brakes, the vehicle swerved into my lane missing my vehicle by two or three inches. It was so close that I remember thinking: If I had one more coat of paint! Had I not obeyed the voice of the Holy Spirit, I would have been forced into the highway divider barrier. The Holy Spirit truly did tell me what was to come.

For us to understand the difference between Logos and Rhema requires us to examine the fruit that each produces. We have discussed the fruit of Logos, but Rhema produces different fruit.

However, before we examine Rhema's fruit, let us first understand how, and when Rhema was used by God in the Old Testament. As we previously discussed, God would often walk in the Garden of Eden and talk to Adam and Eve:

And they heard the sound of the LORD God walking in the garden in the cool of the day, and Adam and his wife hid themselves from the presence of the LORD God among the trees of the garden. 9 Then the LORD God called to Adam and said to him, "Where are you?" 10 So he said, "I heard Your voice in the garden, and I was afraid because I was naked; and I hid myself." Gen. 3:8-10

The word "**sound**", comes from the Hebrew word *qowl,* which means; "to call aloud; a voice or sound" (Strong's). They heard and recognized the voice of God. They did not have the written word, (Logos), at that time. It was not until after God gave Moses the Ten Commandments that men had the Logos of what God said. The rest of the written word, inspired by God, did not come until Moses wrote the first five books known as the Torah.

Furthermore, throughout the Old Testament, God spoke with an audible voice to His prophets and people, just as He did with Moses.

In the New Covenant, God has spoken through His son, Jesus Christ, audibly until the time of His death and in written form afterwards. It should be of no surprise then, that God has chosen to continue to talk to His Church today, using the Holy Spirit. Jesus told us this was what was to come. But, *Rhema* has become one of the least understood Greek words in the Bible today.

Let us examine the word "*Rhema*" more closely. "*Rhema*" is a compound word consisting of two Greek words. The first part is, *rheo* (hreh'-o), and it connotes the idea of pouring forth such as to utter, flow, or run. The second part is, *ma* (-ma), and this ending often carries the force of effect or result (UBS Handbook Series). We can best understand its usage in the Greek word, "*Chrisma*". "Chrisma", is a spiritual endowment, *ma* meaning "*a portion*" of grace. How does this apply to Rhema? Jesus best describes it in John 7:39:

> *On the last day, that great day of the feast, Jesus stood and cried out, saying, "If anyone thirsts, let him come to Me and drink. 38 He who believes in Me, as the Scripture has said,* **out of his heart will flow rivers of living water." 39 But this He spoke concerning the Spirit, whom those believing in Him would receive;** *for the Holy Spirit was not yet given, because Jesus was not yet glorified.*

Jesus is telling us that something is going to flow out of our hearts when we are filled with the Holy Spirit. What is it that will flow? He gives us the answer to this question in Matthew 12: 34-37 in His rebuke of the Scribes and Pharisees:

"Brood of vipers! How can you, being evil, speak good things? For out of the abundance of the heart the mouth speaks. 35 A good man out of the good treasure of his heart brings forth good things, and an evil man out of the evil treasure brings forth evil things.

*36 **But I say to you that for every idle word men may speak, they will give account of it in the Day of Judgment. 37 For by your words you will be justified, and by your words you will be condemned.***"

This passage of scripture is very significant in that it helps us understand the definition of *Rhema*. First, we understand that what treasure we have our hearts filled with will eventually come out of our mouth. A treasure is something on which we put great value. A primary point that Jesus makes here is that it can be good or evil. He goes on to say there will be judgment for what we allow to come forth from our mouth. He said that we shall be judged for every *"idle word"* we speak.

The word "**idle**", comes from the Greek word *argos*, and it means "unprofitable, barren, idle, or useless." *Argos,* references things from which no profit is derived, although they can and ought to be producing fruit, such as fields or trees (Thayer's). However, it is most important for us to note that the, *idle word,* translated here, is *"unprofitable rhema"*.

The Rhema we allow to proceed from our mouth is that which we will be accountable for on the Day of Judgment. **This would indicate that Rhema can be good, or rhema can be bad depending on which spirit we are listening to.** Not only can we be encouraged to speak Rhema words given to us by the Holy Spirit, but we can be enticed to speak rhema words given to us by the demonic spirits. We see a great example of this in Matt 16:13-23:

> *When Jesus came into the region of Caesarea Philippi, He asked His disciples, saying, "Who do men say that I, the Son of Man, am?" 14 So they said, "Some say John the Baptist, some Elijah, and others Jeremiah or one of the prophets." 15 He said to them, "But who do you say that I am?"*

> *16 Simon Peter answered and said, "You are the Christ, the Son of the living God." 17 Jesus answered and said to him, "Blessed are you, Simon Bar-Jonah, for flesh and blood has not revealed this to you, but My Father who is in heaven. 18 And I also say to you that you are Peter, and on this rock I will build My church, and the gates of Hades shall not prevail against it. 19 And I will give you the keys of the kingdom of heaven, and whatever you bind on earth will be bound in heaven, and whatever you loose on earth will be loosed in heaven."*

> *20 Then He commanded His disciples that they should tell no one that He was Jesus the Christ. 21 From that time Jesus began to show to His disciples that He must go to Jerusalem, and suffer many things from the elders and chief priests and scribes, and be killed, and be raised the third day.*

> *22 Then Peter took Him aside and began to rebuke Him, saying, "Far be it from You, Lord; this shall not happen to You!" 23 But He turned and said to Peter,*

*"**Get behind Me, Satan**! You are an offense to Me, for you are not mindful of the things of God, but the things of men."*

Jesus did not say, "Get behind me, Peter." He said, "*Get behind me, Satan*". Jesus was addressing the spirit that enticed Peter to say what he said.

This, in fact, creates a great dilemma for mankind, because there are thousands of voices that speak to us every day, and the one we yield our thoughts and tongue to will dictate what fruit we will enjoy in life. We will reap from the seed type, which we sow. Rhema may come from fellow workers, friends, or family, who mean well, but their words (rhema) do not produce life or agree with the Word (Logos) of God.

This is why Jesus goes on to say in Matthew 12:37,

"by your words (Logos), you will be justified and by your words (logos), you will be condemned."

This also explains how Logos and Rhema work together. The Logos of God is the good treasure that we read, study, and sow into our heart. Remember, Logos produces the fruit of discernment by which we can judge what spirit we are hearing. This is why Paul tells us to take every thought captive to the obedience of Christ, the Logos made flesh. However, as we discussed previously, Logos is the seed that will sprout forth God's Rhema, or Holy Spirit inspired word (Rhema) that will produce life in us.

Jesus tells us in John 6:63,

92

It is the Spirit who gives life; the flesh profits nothing. The words (Rhema) that I speak to you are spirit, and they are life."

It is this Rhema, the sword of the Spirit, our offensive armament that produces life in us, and is to be used against our primary enemy in this life, Satan. In contrast, a defenseless soldier in the war of the spirit realm can become both a pawn and target of the enemy.

CHAPTER 10

THE FRUITS OF RHEMA

Just as we discovered that Logos produces fruit, God continues to implement His plan of producing fruit with Rhema. There are several different types of fruit produced by Rhema.

REVELATION

The first fruit that Rhema produces is **revelation.** What is revelation? Revelation is the uncovering of truth. We see a great example of revelation as we revisit Matthew 16:13-18:

When Jesus came into the region of Caesarea Philippi, He asked His disciples, saying, "Who do men say that I, the Son of Man, am?" 14 So they said, "Some say John the Baptist, some Elijah, and others Jeremiah or one of the prophets." 15 He said to them, "But who do you say that I am?"

*16 Simon Peter answered and said, "You are the Christ, the Son of the living God." 17 Jesus answered and said to him, "Blessed are you, Simon Bar-Jonah, for **flesh and blood has not revealed this to you,** but My Father who is in heaven. 18 And I also say to you that you are Peter, and on this rock I will build My church, and the gates of Hades shall not prevail against it.*

Jesus asked the question, "*Who do men say that I, the son of man, am?*" His disciples replied in verse fourteen, "*Some say John the Baptist, some Elijah, and others Jeremiah or one of the prophets.*" Jesus then goes on to ask, "*Who do you say that I am?*" Note how Simon Peter replies to this question, and Jesus makes a very important statement to him: "*Flesh and blood did not reveal this to you, Peter.*"

If flesh and blood did not reveal this to Peter, who did? Jesus quickly answers His own question. He said, "*my Father (God) revealed this to you, Peter.*" **Note! Jesus did not ask:** "Who do you *think* I am"? He asked, "W*ho do you say that I am*"? Peter's reply was quick and to the point: "*You are the Christ, the Son of the living God.*"

It was a Rhema word, inspired by the Holy Spirit, producing **the fruit of revelation** to Peter and those around him. Jesus then declares that this new process of obtaining revelation will be the rock on which He will build His Church. This is an important passage of scripture for us to understand.

As great a man and disciple as Peter was, of even greater importance to the Church is the revelation of the true identity of Jesus Christ. That is why there is a distinction between the meanings of the two Greek words translated as *Peter* and *petra*. Peter's name *Petros* means "smaller or piece of a rock."

The Greek word "*rock*", that Matthew used to quote Jesus, as He described the foundation of His Church, is the Greek word *Petra,* and it means "a mass or **larger rock**" (Strong's). The Church grows only when people obtain the revelation that **Jesus Christ is their Lord and Savior, and the Rock the Church is built upon.**

People around the world obtain this revelation every day as other Christians speak this Rhema into their lives, and the fruit of revelation produces new converts to the Church. This truth is foremost in the Apostle Paul's letter to the Church in Rome:

> *How then shall they call on Him in whom they have not believed? And how shall they believe in Him of whom they have not heard?* **And how shall they hear without a preacher?** *15 And how shall they preach unless they are sent? As it is written: "How beautiful are the feet of those who preach the gospel of peace, Who bring glad tidings of good things!" 16 But they have not all obeyed the gospel. For Isaiah says, "LORD, who has believed our report?"*

> *17* ***So then faith comes by hearing, and hearing by the word (rhema) of God.*** Romans 10:14 -17 NKJV

Paul goes on to add in Ephesians 1:13,

> *In Him you also trusted,* **after you heard the word (Rhema) of truth,** *the gospel of your salvation; in whom also, having believed, you were sealed with the Holy Spirit of promise, 14 who is the guarantee of our inheritance until the redemption of the purchased possession, to the praise of His glory.*

Not only is it impossible for anyone to be saved until they receive the revelation of who Jesus Christ is through Rhema, **a second fruit** is required and comes only by Rhema.

FAITH

So then, faith comes by hearing, and hearing by the word (Rhema) of God. Rom 10:17

It is important to note that the Greek word translated as, "*God*", in this passage of scripture (NKJV) is actually the Greek word *Christos,* which means "the anointed, i.e. the Messiah, the Christ" (Strong's) and is almost always translated as, "Christ." Several Bible translations make this distinction. I point this out, because it changes the whole understanding of what has been stated by Paul.

Faith will come only when we obtain the revelation of who the Messiah is, and what He has accomplished for us to be saved and redeemed from the curse of spiritual death. It is not enough to have knowledge of God. Israel heard this truth from God Himself in Deuteronomy 32:20 -21:

*And He said, "I will hide My face from them, I will see what their end will be, For they are a perverse generation, **Children in whom is no faith.***

21 They have provoked Me to jealousy by what is not God; They have moved Me to anger by their foolish idols. But I will provoke them to jealousy by those who are not a nation; I will move them to anger by a foolish nation."

The perverse generation God is talking about had knowledge of God, yet God said there was no faith in them. Therefore, we see that it is not enough to know about God, for Apostle James tells us in James 2:19 -20:

You believe that there is one God. You do well. Even the demons believe — and tremble! 20 But do you want to know, O foolish man, that faith without works is dead?

Many people around the world know about the president of the United States, but few people know him personally. Many people believe there is a god, or even gods, but do not know The God.

This is the primary commission of the Church: Go and tell people how to enter the Kingdom of God. It was the primary mission Jesus had, and it is our mission today. Jesus said in Luke 4:43, *"I must preach the kingdom of God to the other cities also, because for this purpose I have been sent."*

The kingdom of God is a kingdom of relationship based on son-ship. When we hear the Rhema (word) and obtain the revelation of our salvation, our faith will grow in Christ, and we will walk in the fullness of what Jesus has provided for us: healing, prosperity, deliverance, safety, and preservation. This truth is of critical importance to the church, for the writer of Hebrews 11:5 -7 tells us,

But without faith it is impossible to please Him, for he who comes to God must believe that He is, and that He is a rewarder of those who diligently seek Him.

This statement tells us that without the fruit of Rhema, (faith), we receive nothing from God. How critical is Rhema in our life? Our well-being and life depend upon it. We cannot have faith without Rhema. **Faith comes by Rhema**. This has become a major issue in the Church. There are many

Christians today that are hoping for things from God, but they have no Rhema, nor faith, to receive from God.

SPIRITUAL UNDERSTANDING

This brings us to the third fruit. What is the third fruit of Rhema? The third fruit produced by Rhema is "**Spiritual Understanding**". What is Spiritual Understanding? Spiritual Understanding is seeing things as God see them. We see several examples of this truth in Luke: 2:49-50:

> *And He said to them, "Why did you seek Me? Did you not know that I must be about My Father's business?" 50 But they did not understand the <u>statement</u> (Rhema) which He spoke to them.*

The word "*statement*", is translated from the Greek word *Rhema,* in this passage, and the word "*sayings*", is also translated from *Rhema* in this next passage.

> *And they were all amazed at the majesty of God. But while everyone marveled at all the things which Jesus did, He said to His disciples, 44 "Let these words sink down into your ears, for the Son of Man is about to be betrayed into the hands of men." 45 But **they did not understand this saying (Rhema),** and it was hidden from them so that they did not perceive it; and they were afraid to ask Him about this saying.* Luke 9:43-45

It is not until later that Jesus opened their spiritual ears to hear what He was saying, and for them to obtain spiritual understanding:

Then He said to them, "These are the words which I spoke to you while I was still with you, that all things must be fulfilled which were written in the Law of Moses and the Prophets and the Psalms concerning Me." 45 And **He opened their understanding,** *that they might comprehend the Scriptures.* Luke 24:44-45

It is several years later in Paul's letter to the church at Ephesus, that he prays this prayer for the church:

Therefore I also, after I heard of your faith in the Lord Jesus and your love for all the saints, 16 do not cease to give thanks for you, making mention of you in my prayers: 17 that the God of our Lord Jesus Christ, the Father of glory, **may give to you the spirit of wisdom and revelation in the knowledge of Him, 18 the eyes of your understanding being enlightened; that you may know what is the hope of His calling, what are the riches of the glory of His inheritance in the saints,** *19 and what is the exceeding greatness of His power toward us who believe, according to the working of His mighty power 20 which He worked in Christ when He raised Him from the dead and seated Him at His right hand in the heavenly places, 21 far above all principality and power and might and dominion, and every name that is named, not only in this age but also in that which is to come.* Eph. 1:15-21

It is only after the disciples received **spiritual understanding** that they comprehended God's plan and purpose for all of mankind through His son, Jesus Christ. This also explains the significance of Rhema when Jesus said:

"It is the Spirit who gives life; the flesh profits nothing. **The words (Rhema) that I speak to you are spirit, and they are life.** *64 But there are some of you who do not believe."* John 6: 63-64

I believe this statement could have been one of the great inspirations for Paul to write Romans 10: 8-10:

But what does it say? "The word (Rhema) is near you, in your mouth and in your heart" (that is, the word (Rhema) of faith which we preach): 9 that if you confess with your mouth the Lord Jesus and believe in your heart that God has raised Him from the dead, you will be saved (Verb). 10 For with the heart one believes unto righteousness, and with the mouth confession is made unto salvation (Noun).

The very revelation of this statement has brought multitudes into the Kingdom of God, and it is important to note the completeness of what Rhema supplies. The word *"saved"*, comes from the Greek word *sozo,* which means; "deliverance, safety, healing, prosperity and preservation." However, *sozo,* is a verb, which means "a process or the action of being delivered, saved, healed, prosperity, and preservation."

As we read this passage in Romans 10: 8, we see that there is a process for being saved. We must confess with our mouth, and believe in our hearts. Rhema is constantly working in us to bring us to the point of salvation. Salvation becomes the end-result of what we believe and speak. *"Salvation"*, translates from the Greek word *soteria,* which is a noun. We remember that a noun is a person, place, or thing. It is something that we can experience, something that we can take hold of or grasp.

The Greek definition of *"soteria"*, means; "safety, deliverance, healing, prosperity, and preservation." Therefore, to expound on what this passage is saying, it is the Rhema of God, producing faith, which works in us to bring complete spiritual understanding of salvation (safety, deliverance, healing, prosperity, and preservation) into our lives.

Too many in the Church today do not understand what Jesus has provided for His Church. Many in the Church believe salvation pertains only to our future, when we die and enter heaven. However, the apostle Paul declares in 2 Corinthians 6:2, *"Behold, now is the accepted time; behold, now is the day of salvation"*. If salvation, as Paul states, is today, then healing is today; safety is today; prosperity is today; deliverance is today; and preservation is today - not just when we die and get to heaven.

Why are Rhema and Logos so important to the Church today? Jesus tells us in Luke 4:4:

But Jesus answered him, saying, "It is written, 'Man shall not live by bread (Logos) alone, but by every word (Rhema) of God.'"

It is the two working together that produces the fullness of what Jesus has supplied through salvation to the church.

CHAPTER 11

THE KEYS TO THE KINGDOM

"And I will give you the keys of the kingdom of heaven, and whatever you bind on earth will be bound in heaven, and, whatever, you loose on earth, will be loosed in heaven." 20 Then He commanded His disciples that they should tell no one that He was Jesus the Christ. 21 From that time Jesus began to show to His disciples that He must go to Jerusalem, and suffer many things from the elders and chief priests and scribes, and be killed, and be raised the third day. Matt. 16:19 -21

One of the great debates in Church history is: What are the keys to the Kingdom of God? One thing should be obvious: The keys pertain to - words. Jesus said, *"My words (Rhema) are spirit and they are life to those who find them."* **Words are the only things that we have to transcend the boundaries separating the physical world from the spiritual world.** This is why Proverbs 18:21 tells us that, *"life and death are in the power of the tongue."*

As discussed earlier, our words have the power to set the very course of our future. The Rhema that we speak will either bind or loosen things on Earth or in the heavenlies. I need to point out that the Greek word translated as *"heaven"*, is also translated as, *heavenlies.* This would better define the power of words. The heavenlies, define the entire spiritual dimension, or realm, that we live in and surrounds us. Not only do our words bind and loose heaven, but they can bind and loosen the heavenlies. How can words affect heaven? Jesus tells us in John 15:7 -8,

"If you abide in Me, and My words (Rhema) abide in you, you will ask what you desire, and it shall be done for you. 8 By this My Father is glorified, that you bear much fruit; so you will be My disciples."

If we move and have our being in Him, and His Rhema (revelation, spiritual understanding, and faith) lives in us, then we can ask for what we desire and heaven will move (be loosed) to do it. We also have the ability to bind the works of the enemy. This why Paul tells us in Eph 6:12 -13:

For we do not wrestle against flesh and blood, but against principalities, against powers, against the rulers of the darkness of this age, against spiritual hosts of wickedness in the heavenly places.

Therefore, we must also consider the alternative results to whatever we bind or loose in the heavenlies, for it will also come to pass. If the Rhema we speak moves the heavenlies, then it can also move hell. This is how life and death are in the power of the tongue. The Rhema/rhema that we speak empowers either angels or demons to move on the basis of what we say. This explains why we will be accountable for every Rhema/rhema ((Holy Spirit inspired (Rhema)/ or demonic inspired (rhema)) that proceeds from our mouths (Matt.12: 36).

A great example of this accountability for our words can be read in Numbers twenty-two. This chapter in Numbers is the story of a fearful king, by the name of Balak, who sends for a man named Balaam to speak a curse on Israel. It is evident that Balaam had the ability to speak curses upon people, and have his words come to pass. Balak's request of Balaam is written in verses 5 -6:

*"Look, a people has come from Egypt. See, they cover the face of the earth, and are settling next to me! 6 Therefore please come at once, curse this people for me, for they are too mighty for me. Perhaps I shall be able to defeat them and drive them out of the land, for **I know that he whom you bless is blessed, and he whom you curse is cursed**."*

It would be easy to think that this ability to curse was nothing but a fable, however; God thought enough of it to send an angel to stop it from happening. We read about God's response in Numbers 22: 9 -12,

*Then God came to Balaam and said, "Who are these men with you?" 10 So Balaam said to God, "Balak the son of Zippor, king of Moab, has sent to me, saying, 11 'Look, a people has come out of Egypt, and they cover the face of the earth. Come now, curse them for me; perhaps I shall be able to overpower them and drive them out.'" 12 And God said to Balaam, "You shall not go with them; **you shall not curse the people, for they are blessed**."*

The fact that Balaam's words could have such a negative effect on Israel stirred God to the point of anger.

*Then **God's anger was aroused** because he went, and the Angel of the LORD took His stand in the way as an adversary against him. And he was riding on his*

donkey, and his two servants were with him. 23 Now the donkey saw the Angel of the LORD standing in the way with His drawn sword in His hand, and the donkey turned aside out of the way and went into the field. So Balaam struck the donkey to turn her back onto the road.

24 Then the Angel of the LORD stood in a narrow path between the vineyards, with a wall on this side and a wall on that side. 25 And when the donkey saw the Angel of the LORD, she pushed herself against the wall and crushed Balaam's foot against the wall; so he struck her again. 26 Then the Angel of the LORD went further, and stood in a narrow place where there was no way to turn either to the right hand or to the left.

27 And when the donkey saw the Angel of the LORD, she lay down under Balaam; so Balaam's anger was aroused, and he struck the donkey with his staff. 28 Then the LORD opened the mouth of the donkey, and she said to Balaam, "What have I done to you, that you have struck me these three times?" 29 And Balaam said to the donkey, "Because you have abused me. I wish there were a sword in my hand, for now I would kill you!"

30 So the donkey said to Balaam, "Am I not your donkey on which you have ridden, ever since I became yours, to this day? Was I ever disposed to do this to you?" And he said, "No."

31 **Then the LORD opened Balaam's eyes, and he saw the Angel of the LORD standing in the way with His drawn sword in His hand; and he bowed his head and**

fell flat on his face. 32 And the Angel of the LORD said to him, "Why have you struck your donkey these three times? Behold, I have come out to stand against you, **because your way is perverse before Me.**

33 The donkey saw Me and turned aside from Me these three times. If she had not turned aside from Me, surely I would also have killed you by now, and let her live." 34 And Balaam said to the Angel of the LORD, "I have sinned, for I did not know You stood in the way against me. Now therefore, if it displeases You, I will turn back." Num. 22: 22 -34

It is evident that the prospective power of Balaam's words moved God to a point of action to stop him from prophesying anything negative against God's people, Israel.

Is it any different for us today? Our words will also produce results, be it life, or death. Our words are the keys that open or close the gates of heaven, or hell, and we will have accountability for what proceeds out of our mouth.

No one describes the power of the tongue better than James, as he writes in James 3:1-12:

My brethren, let not many of you become teachers, knowing that we shall receive a stricter judgment. 2 For we all stumble in many things. If anyone does not stumble in word, he is a perfect man, able also to bridle the whole body. 3 Indeed, we put bits in horses' mouths that they may obey us, and we turn their whole body. 4 Look also at ships: although they are so large and are driven by fierce winds, they are turned by a very small rudder wherever the pilot desires. 5 Even so the tongue is a little member and boasts great things. See how great a forest a little fire kindles!

6 And the tongue is a fire, a world of iniquity. **The tongue is so set among our members that it defiles the whole body, and sets on fire the course of nature; and it is set on fire by hell.** *7 For every kind of beast and bird, of reptile and creature of the sea, is tamed and has been tamed by mankind. 8 But no man can tame the tongue. It is an unruly evil, full of deadly poison. 9 With it we bless our God and Father, and with it we curse men, who have been made in the similitude of God.*

10 Out of the same mouth proceed blessing and cursing. My brethren, these things ought not to be so. 11 Does a spring send forth fresh water and bitter from the same opening? 12 Can a fig tree, my brethren, bear olives, or a grapevine bear figs? Thus no spring yields both salt water and fresh.

James tells us that, *"no man can tame the tongue."* The Greek word for *"tame"*, is, *damazo (dam-ad'-zo),* and it means; 'to restrain, or curb' (Thayer's). Does this mean that the tongue cannot be controlled? No! It simply means that it cannot be controlled by man. However, the tongue can be controlled by the greater one that dwells in us, the Holy Spirit.

Peter would not have given us this word of encouragement if it were not possible to obtain, as 1 Peter 3: 8 -12 tells us,

Finally, all of you be of one mind, having compassion for one another; love as brothers, be tenderhearted, be courteous; 9 not returning evil for evil or reviling for

110

reviling, but on the contrary blessing, knowing that you were called to this, that you may inherit a blessing. 10 For **"He who would love life And see good days, Let him refrain his tongue from evil, And his lips from speaking deceit.** *11 Let him turn away from evil and do good; Let him seek peace and pursue it. 12 For the eyes of the LORD are on the righteous, And His ears are open to their prayers; But the face of the LORD is against those who do evil."*

It is not only the job of the Holy Spirit to speak to us, repeating and revealing what God says, but He can also help us control what words proceed out of our mouth.

CHAPTER 12

Has The Brook Dried Up?

1 Kings 17:1-7

*Now Elijah the Tishbite, who was of the settlers of Gilead, said to Ahab, "As the Lord, the God of Israel lives, before whom I stand, surely there shall be neither dew nor rain these years, except by my word." 2 The word of the Lord came to him, saying, 3 "Go away from here and turn eastward, and hide yourself by the brook Cherith, which is east of the Jordan. 4 "It shall be that you will drink of the brook, and **I have commanded the ravens to provide for you there." 5 So he went and did according to the word of the Lord, for he went and lived by the brook Cherith**, which is east of the Jordan. 6 The ravens brought him bread and meat in the morning and bread and meat in the evening, and he would drink from the brook. 7 **It happened after a while that the brook dried up, because there was no rain in the land.***

In the years before Elijah's ministry, we discover King Ahab had introduced the worship of false gods and idols in Israel.

1 Kings 16:31-34

It came about, as though it had been a trivial thing for him to walk in the sins of Jeroboam the son of Nebat, that he married Jezebel the daughter of Ethbaal king of the Sidonians, and went to serve Baal and worshiped him. 32 So he erected an altar for Baal in the house of Baal which he built in Samaria. 33 Ahab also made the Asherah. Thus Ahab did more to provoke the Lord God of Israel than all the kings of Israel who were before him.

This is the very thing God warned Israel against in Deuteronomy 11:16-17;

Take heed to yourselves, lest your heart be deceived, and you turn aside and serve other gods and worship them, lest the Lord's anger be aroused against you, and He shut up the heavens so that there be no rain, and the land yield no produce, and you perish quickly from the good land which the LORD is giving you.

These acts of idolatry, prompted Elijah to prophesy that no dew or rain would fall on the land for years. It was after this proclamation (Rhema) that God tells Elijah to go to the **Brook Cherith. Why is this important to us today?**

The English word, **Cherith**, comes from the Hebrew name, *Keriyth (ker-eeth')* which means to cut. It originates from the Hebrew root word, **karath (kaw-rath'),** which means; **to covenant** (i.e. make an alliance or bargain, originally by cutting flesh and passing between the pieces). As we know from history, God always provided for His people through His covenant. With this definition and understanding in mind, we can read this passage of Scripture in this manner.

1 Kings 17:1-7

*Now Elijah the Tishbite, who was of the settlers of Gilead, said to Ahab, "As the Lord, the God of Israel lives, before whom I stand, surely there shall be neither dew nor rain these years, except by my word." 2 The word of the Lord came to him, saying, 3 "Go away from here and turn eastward, and hide yourself **in the Covenant (brook Cherith)**, which is east of the Jordan. 4 "It shall be that you* *will drink of the brook, and **I have commanded the ravens to provide** (Covenant provision) for you there." 5 So he went and did according to the word of the Lord, for he went and lived in the Covenant (brook Cherith), which is east of the Jordan. 6 The ravens brought him bread and meat in the morning and bread and meat in the evening, and he would drink from the Covenant (brook). 7 **It happened after a while that the brook dried up, because there was no rain in the land.***

God met every need Elijah had through His Covenant. However, there came a time when the provision dried up. This prompts the question: **Why did the brook dry up?** The answer is simple…there was no rain in the land. It is now that we discover there are two types of rain referenced in the Bible.

Joel 2:23-26

*So rejoice, O sons of Zion, And be glad in the Lord your God; For He has given you **the early rain** for your vindication. And He has poured down for you the rain, **The early and latter rain** as before. 24 The threshing floors will be full of grain, And the vats will overflow with the new wine and oil. 25 "Then I will make up to you for the years That the swarming locust has eaten, The creeping locust, the stripping locust and the gnawing locust, My great army which I sent among you. 26 "You will have plenty to eat and be satisfied*

It is here that we must note the obvious; rain is water, and water is symbolic of the Rhema of God. The Apostle Paul gives us this revelation in Eph 5:25-28:

*Husbands love your wives, just as Christ also loved the church and gave Himself up for her, 26 so that He might sanctify her, **having***

cleansed her by the washing of water with the word (Rhema), *27 that He might present to Himself the church in all her glory, having no spot or wrinkle or any such thing; but that she would be holy and blameless.*

With this definition, we can gain new understanding of several passages of scripture:

1 John 5:5-9

*Who is the one who overcomes the world, but he who believes that Jesus is the Son of God? 6 This is the One who came by water (Rhema) and blood, Jesus Christ; not with the water (Rhema) only, but with the water (Rhema) and with the blood. It is the Spirit who testifies, because the Spirit is the truth. 7 For there are three that testify: 8 **the Spirit** and the water **(the Rhema)** and **the blood**; and the three are in agreement.*

Heb 10:19-23

*Therefore, brethren, since we have confidence to enter the holy place by the blood of Jesus, 20 by a new and living way which He inaugurated for us through the veil, that is, His flesh, 21 and since we have a great priest over the house of God, 22 **let us draw near with a sincere heart in full assurance of faith, having our hearts sprinkled clean from an evil conscience and our bodies washed with pure water (the Rhema).***

John 4:7-14

*There came a woman of Samaria to draw water. Jesus said to her, **"Give Me a drink."** 8 For His disciples had gone away into the city to buy food. 9 Therefore the Samaritan woman said to Him, "How is it that You, being a Jew, ask me for a drink since I am a*

*Samaritan woman?" (For Jews have no dealings with Samaritans.)
10 Jesus answered and said to her, "If you knew the gift of God,
and who it is who says to you, 'Give Me a drink,' you would have
asked Him, and He would have given you **living water**." 11 She
said to Him, "Sir, You have nothing to draw with and the well is
deep; where then do You get that **living water**? 12 "You are not
greater than our father Jacob, are You, who gave us the well, and
drank of it himself and his sons and his cattle?" 13 Jesus answered
and said to her, "Everyone who drinks of this **water** will thirst
again; 14 but whoever drinks of the **water (the Rhema)** that I will
give him shall never thirst; but the **water (the Rhema)** that I will
give him will become in him a well of **water (Rhema)** springing up
to eternal life."*

Jesus' reply to the Samaritan woman is simply that the provision of
the Old Covenant water to Jacob will not satisfy the thirst in a man's
heart. Only the Rhema (water) of the New Covenant in Jesus Christ
will spring up eternal life.

We now also gain the understanding as to why the provision of
covenant for Elijah came to a stop. Elijah as the prophet of God, was
the voice of God, speaking Rhema across the land. When he ceased to
water the land with the Rhema of God, the land dried up and all
provision ceased.

Matt 4:4

*But He answered and said, "It is written, 'MAN SHALL NOT LIVE
ON BREAD ALONE, BUT ON EVERY **WORD (Rhema)** THAT
PROCEEDS OUT OF THE MOUTH OF GOD.'"*

Has your brook dried up? And are you not seeing the provisions of
God's covenant in your life? Could it be that you have stopped seeking

the Kingdom of God first, and the rain has ceased. This was the situation that Ezra confronted with Israel! They found their answer at the Water Gate.

Neh 8:1-8

> *And **all the people gathered as one man at the square which was in front of the Water Gate**, and they asked Ezra the scribe to bring the book of the law of Moses which the Lord had given to Israel. 2 **Then Ezra the priest brought the law before the assembly of men, women and all who could listen with understanding, on the first day of the seventh month.** 3 He read from it before the square which was in front of **the Water Gate** from early morning until midday, in the presence of men and women, those who could understand; and all the people were attentive to the book of the law. 4 Ezra the scribe stood at a wooden podium which they had made for the purpose. And beside him stood Mattithiah, Shema, Anaiah, Uriah, Hilkiah, and Maaseiah on his right hand; and Pedaiah, Mishael, Malchijah, Hashum, Hashbaddanah, Zechariah and Meshullam on his left hand. 5 Ezra opened the book in the sight of all the people for he was standing above all the people; and when he opened it, all the people stood up. 6 Then Ezra blessed the Lord the great God. And all the people answered, "Amen, Amen!" while lifting up their hands; then they bowed low and worshiped the Lord with their faces to the ground. 7 Also Jeshua, Bani, Sherebiah, Jamin, Akkub, Shabbethai, Hodiah, Maaseiah, Kelita, Azariah, Jozabad, Hanan, Pelaiah, the Levites, explained the law to the people while the people remained in their place. 8 They read from the book, from the law of God, translating to give the sense so that they understood the reading.*

When the Rhema (and its fruit of revelation) is not coming forth, the land will dry up and the provision will stop. However, if we continue in God's word (the Logos), the Rhema will sprout forth; its fruit of revelation will continue to come down, and we will see prosperity in every area of our life.

Mark 4:26-29

> *And He was saying, "The kingdom of God is like a man who casts seed (Logos) upon the soil; 27 and he goes to bed at night and gets up by day, and the seed (Logos) sprouts and grows — how, he himself does not know. 28 "The soil produces crops by itself; first the blade, then the head, then the mature grain in the head. 29 "But when the crop permits, he immediately puts in the sickle, because the harvest (Rhema) has come."*

CHAPTER 13

GOD, ARE YOU TALKING?

In this book, we have explored the ways God has communicated with His people. As we have discovered, His methods are no different today, from how He has talked to people throughout mankind's history.

The issue has never been one of, 'does God speak to His people today': but of greater concern: Do people have ears to hear? God has always communicated with His people, and that has not changed today. However, with the busy hectic lives that we live, hearing is the primary problem.

Do you want to hear the voice of God? What are you willing to do to hear Him? Is it worth sowing time with Him to learn and discern His voice?

And Jesus said to them, "I am the bread of life. He who comes to Me shall never hunger, and he who believes in Me shall never thirst." John 6:35

We are not the only ones to have experienced the problem of hearing. There was a time when the disciples were so enamored with what was going on around them that they had the same issue, even while in the presence of the Son of God:

But while everyone marveled at all the things which Jesus did, He said to His disciples, 44 "Let these words sink down into your ears, for the Son of Man is about to be betrayed into the hands of men." 45 But they did not understand this saying (Rhema), and it was hidden from them so that they did not perceive it; and they were afraid to ask Him about this saying. Luke 9: 43 -45

The simple truth is this: The Holy Spirit of God wants to talk to you today. Will you give (sow) Him the time to listen?

After spending time with Jesus, He opened the ears and eyes of understanding for the disciples in Luke 24: 44 -45:

*Then He said to them, "These are the words (Logos) which I spoke to you while I was still with you, that all things must be fulfilled which were written in the Law of Moses and the Prophets and the Psalms concerning Me." 45 And **He opened their understanding, that they might comprehend the Scriptures.***

This world has many voices talking and calling us every day. A great example of many voices is the radio. If we turn on the radio and move across the dial, we can hear many different voices. But, how many people have a favorite national syndicated radio show that they listen to? If you travel across America, from city to city, you will turn from one radio station to another radio station until you hear that familiar voice. How is it that you recognize that voice? You recognize that voice because of the time you spend listening to it at home or work. Through fellowship, you have established a connection with that radio host.

A mother can recognize her crying child from anywhere, because she knows its cry. Why? She has spent hours with her child. She has established fellowship and relationship with that child.

Herein lies the answer to obtaining spiritual understanding and the knowledge of God's ways, The most important time we spend every day is the time we spend at the feet of Jesus; seeing, reading, and hearing with our spiritual eyes and ears, His words (Logos and Rhema) of life.

Both, Rhema and Logos, are about relationship established through fellowship. We have neither, unless we sow the seed of time. Without a sowing, there is no harvest. Without sowing time into a relationship, there is no fellowship obtained. This brings us to a very important point.

What distinguishes the Christian from all the other religions of the world? For many, this can be a very complex question, and as we know, it has even created many different denominations in the Christian faith. However, there is one word in the English language that helps define Christianity, yet at the same time creates confusion in the religious world. In English, that word is '*know*'.

The English word "*know*" *is* translated 964 times in the Bible. This in itself would not be confusing except that the word, *know* has several different meanings and is translated from three Hebrew words and six Greek words that all express different meanings for the word, *know*.

Synonyms for the word, *know,* are translated hundreds of additional times. This is why the English dictionary defines *know,* in several ways as follows:

Know | nō | verb (past **knew** | n(y)oō | ; past part. **known** | nōn |):

1. Be aware of through observation, inquiry, or information, have knowledge or information concerning, be absolutely certain or sure about something.

2.   Have developed a relationship with (someone) through meeting and spending time with them; be familiar or friendly with, have a good command of (a subject or language); recognize (someone or something); be familiar or acquainted with (something); have personal experience of (an emotion or situation); to regard or perceive as having a specified characteristic; give (someone or something) a particular name or title; be able to distinguish one person or thing from (another).

3.   Archaic have sexual intercourse with (someone). [ORIGIN: a Hebraism that has passed into modern language.]

Is it any wonder that when we say we, *know,* someone or something, it can be defined or perceived in several different ways? Here are the three Hebrew words translated as *know*.

1.   **Yada`** (yaw-dah'); (used 941 times) a primitive root: to know (properly, to ascertain by seeing); used in a great variety of senses, figuratively, literally, euphemistically and inferentially (including observation, care, recognition; and causatively, instruction, designation, punishment, etc.) [as follow]: acknowledge, acquaintance (-ted with), advise, answer, appoint, assuredly, be aware, comprehend, consider, cunning, declare, be diligent, (can, cause to) discern, discover, endued with, familiar friend, famous, feel, can have, instruct, kinsfolk, kinsman, (cause to let, make) know, (come to give, have, take) knowledge, have [knowledge], (be, make, make to be, make self) known, be learned, lie by man, mark, perceive, privy to, prognosticator, regard, have respect, skillful, shew, can (man of) skill, be sure, of a surety, teach, (can) tell, understand, have [understanding] (Strong's).

2. **Nakar** (naw-kar'); (used 49 times) a primitive root; properly, to scrutinize, i.e. look intently at; hence (with recognition implied), to acknowledge, be acquainted with, care for, respect, revere, or (with suspicion implied), to disregard, ignore, be strange toward, reject, resign, dissimulate (as if ignorant or disowning) (Strong's).

3. **Da`ath** (dah'-ath); (used 96 times) means; knowledge; cunning, awareness (wittingly) (Strong's).

Someone may ask: Why is it important to understand all these words? Throughout the entire Old Covenant, there is not a single instance where it tells us that a man *knew* God in the same manner that the New Covenant tells us that every Christian should *know* God.

The Bible does tell us that God *knew* several men, such as Abraham in a personal way.

Gen 18:17-20

> *And the Lord said, "Shall I hide from Abraham what I am doing, 18 since Abraham shall surely become a great and mighty nation, and all the nations of the earth shall be blessed in him? 19 **For I have known (yada) him**, in order that he may command his children and his household after him, that they keep the way of the Lord, to do righteousness and justice, that the Lord may bring to Abraham what He has spoken to him."*

Exodus 33:11-23,

> *So the Lord spoke to Moses face to face, **as a man speaks to his friend**. And he would return to the camp, but his servant Joshua the son of Nun, a young man, did not depart from the tabernacle. 12 Then Moses said*

to the Lord, "See, You say to me, 'Bring up this people.' But You have not let me **know** whom You will send with me. Yet You have said, 'I **know (yada)** you by name, and you have also found grace in My sight.'

13 Now therefore, I pray, **if I have found grace in Your sight, show me now Your way, that I may know (yada) You** *and that I may find grace in Your sight. And consider that this nation is Your people." 14 And He said, "My Presence will go with you, and I will give you rest." 15 Then he said to Him, "If Your Presence does not go with us, do not bring us up from here. 16 For how then will it be* **known (yada)** *that Your people and I have found grace in Your sight, except You go with us? So we shall be separate, Your people and I, from all the people who are upon the face of the earth."*

17 So the Lord said to Moses, "I will also do this thing that you have spoken; for you have found grace in My sight, and **I know (yada) you by name**." *18 And he said, "Please, show me Your glory." 19 Then He said, "I will make all My goodness pass before you, and I will proclaim the name of the Lord before you. I will be gracious to whom I will be gracious, and I will have compassion on whom I will have compassion."*

20 But He said, **"You cannot see My face; for no man shall see Me, and live."** *21 And the Lord said, "Here is a place by Me, and you shall stand on the rock. 22 So it shall be, while My glory passes by, that I will put you in the cleft of the rock, and will cover you with My hand while I pass by. 23 Then I will take away My hand, and you shall see My back;* **but My face shall not be seen."**

The highest status that someone could obtain with God through the Old Covenant was friendship. This friendship was established through Covenant, by faith, and the blood of animal sacrifices. Therefore, a better way and a new relationship would be introduced through the blood of a Better Sacrifice. Jesus Christ gives the Christian a different understanding of *knowing* God.

John 14:7

> *"If you had **known** Me, you would have **known** My Father also; and **from now on you know Him and have seen Him.**"*

With this statement, Jesus establishes a turning point in human history, an event that will change the destiny of mankind for all eternity. This will all happen based on the word, *know*. What does this word mean in the original text, and **why is it so important to us?**

Rhema and Logos are means by which God communicates with His people, and this connection is established through fellowship and relationship. God communicates with those that He **knows**.

The word, *know,* as translated here, comes from the Greek word, *ginosko* (ghin-oce'-ko), which is a primary verb meaning; to "know" (absolutely), understand completely, or to have a complete intimate knowledge.

The Greek-English Lexicon explains it this way: To learn to know a person through direct personal experience, implying a continuity of relationship; to know, to become acquainted with, to be familiar with. It is important to avoid an expression, which will mean merely 'to learn about.' Here the emphasis must be on **the interpersonal relationship, which is experienced.** *Ginosko*, would be used to describe an intimate relationship between married couples.

Jesus is telling His Church that we are entering into something that we never had before, **a relationship with God.** This is all made possible, not because God changed positions, but because Jesus changed ours. In fact, the Apostle Paul tells us that we are unique, that we are *a new creation*.

2 Cor 5:17-18

> *Therefore, if anyone is in Christ,* **he is a new creation;** *old things have passed away; behold, all things have become new.*

This term, *new creation,* actually means something that did not exist before this time. This statement points to the uniqueness of Christianity, and three words that we should take into consideration – **relationship, fellowship, and friendship.**

One of the great misunderstandings in the Church over the centuries stems from the confusion between the words relationship, fellowship, and friendship.

In the English language, these words have become interchangeable in their usage. Due to this mixing together, it has caused great debate, and questions such as: Can a backslider lose their salvation? If once saved, are they forever saved? Does Grace only work once? Does Grace mean we have a license to sin without ramifications? As for a question related to this book: **Does God only talk to His church or everyone?**

Much of the confusion for the answers to these questions derives from this mixing together of the meanings for these words, relationship, fellowship and friendship. So a primary question is: How are these words defined today, and what has changed from their meaning over the years?

Here is how the dictionary defines **relationship**:

Relationship: the way in which two or more concepts, objects, or people are connected, or the state of being connected; the state of being connected by blood or marriage; the way in which two or more people or organizations regard and behave toward each other; an emotional and sexual association between two people.

Now this is the dictionary's definition for **fellowship**: **1.** Friendly association, esp. with people who share one's interests. • A group of people meeting to pursue a shared interest or aim; a guild or corporation.

2. An endowment established or a sum of money awarded to support a scholar or student engaged in advanced research in a particular field.

There appears to be a distinct difference between the definitions of these two words, that is, until we add a third word, **friendship**. Note, the thesaurus combines the two words relationship and fellowship for the meaning of friendship:

1. *Lasting friendships* **relationship**, close **relationship**, attachment, mutual attachment, association, bond, tie, link, union.

2. *Old ties of love and friendship* amity, camaraderie, friendliness, comradeship, companionship, **fellowship**, fellow feeling, **closeness**, affinity, rapport, understanding, harmony, **unity**; **intimacy**, mutual affection, antonym enmity.

By now you may be asking, what does this have to do with anything spiritual? Everything! To understand these words from their original Hebrew and Greek meaning, answers all the above questions and more. Let us first consider the original Hebrew word for relationship.

Relationship comes for the Hebrew root word, *ga'al (gaw-al')*, and it means; to redeem (according to the Oriental law of kinship), i.e. **to be the next of kin** (and as such to buy back a relative's property, marry his widow, etc.): avenger, deliver, kinsfolk (-man), purchase, ransom, redeem (-er), revenger (Strongs). This includes the connection by blood or marriage, such as wife, husband, father, mother, sister, brother and all the grandparents, aunts and uncles and cousins. What is important to note, is that it denotes someone in a fixed position or state of being.

Ga'al, includes a position obtained and maintained through the bloodline, and most important to us, it includes those that have entered a **blood covenant relationship through Jesus Christ**. This is where the blood of two people is mixed together and they become one (Gen. 2:24).

Why the blood? *"The life of the flesh is in the blood",* and by mixing the blood of the two lives together it puts them in a relationship (Lev.17:11).

The Greek word, most often used to define "**relationship**", comes from the word **adelphos** (ad-el-fos'), and its root word, *delphus,* meaning; (the womb); a brother (literally or figuratively). This word is used 343 times in the New Testament. We find one of the most compelling usages in Matt 12:46-50:

*While He was still talking to the multitudes, behold, His mother and brothers stood outside, seeking to speak with Him. 47 Then one said to Him, "Look, Your mother and Your **brothers** are standing outside, seeking to speak with You." 48 But He answered and said to the one who told Him, "Who is My mother and who are My brothers?" 49 And He stretched out His hand toward His disciples and said, "Here are My mother and My **brothers!** 50 For whoever does the will of My Father in heaven is My **brother** and sister and mother."*

I cannot express enough how important it is to understand the difference between these three words; relationship, fellowship, and friendship? It is because fellowship and friendship can be broken, but we are in a fixed position in our relationship with family.

Anyone can lose a friendship or break fellowship with someone they have known. however; **you do not** *lose* **a relationship because they are family.** The relationship is a connection by blood. Although we have a relationship with a brother, sister or other relative, it does not mean we automatically have fellowship with them.

So let us understand this word *"fellowship"* better. The Hebrew word for *"**fellowship",*** is *chabar* (khaw-bar'), It is a primitive root that means; to unite, to join, to bind together, to be joined, to be coupled, to be in league, to heap up, to have fellowship with, to be compact, to be a charmer (Brown-Drivers-Briggs). What is interesting about this word, *chabar* (khaw-bar'), is that it depicts an established principle such as a common cause, interest or goal between the people in fellowship. This explains why fellowship is often broken when common interest changes.

The Greek word for, **fellowship,** is *koinonia* (koy-nohn-ee'-ah), and it means partnership, i.e. (literally) participation, or (social) intercourse, or (pecuniary) benefaction; (to) communicate (-ation), communion, (contri-) distribution, fellowship (Strong's). It is used nineteen times in the New Testament, most often as fellowship, but also as *communion*. Paul uses this term in Phil 3:10-11:

> *That I may __know__ Him and the power of His resurrection, and the __fellowship__ of His sufferings, being conformed to His death, 11 if, by any means, I may attain to the resurrection from the dead.* NKJV

Koinonia (koy-nohn-ee'-ah) is translated differently in 1 Cor 10:16:

> *The cup of blessing which we bless, is it not the* ***communion (koinonia) of the blood of Christ?*** *The bread which we break,* ***is it not the communion (koinonia) of the body of Christ?*** KJV

Why is it imperative that we understand the difference between these words? As a Christian it is possible to break *fellowship* with anyone, even God. However, breaking fellowship or friendship does not mean you break relationship. When we sin, we break our communion *(koinonia)* with God, not our relationship with our Father. One of the great examples of this is given in Luke 15:11-32:

> *Then He said: "A certain man had two sons. 12 And the younger of them said to his father, 'Father, give me the portion of goods that falls to me.' So he divided to*

them his livelihood. 13 And not many days after, the younger son gathered all together, journeyed to a far country, and there wasted his possessions with prodigal living.

14 But when he had spent all, there arose a severe famine in that land, and he began to be in want. 15 Then he went and joined himself to a citizen of that country, and he sent him into his fields to feed swine. 16 And he would gladly have filled his stomach with the pods that the swine ate, and no one gave him anything.

*17 "But **when he came to himself,** he said, 'How many of my father's hired servants have bread enough and to spare, and I perish with hunger! 18 I will arise and go to **my father,** and will say to him, "Father, I have sinned against heaven and before you, 19 and **I am no longer worthy to be called your son.** Make me like one of your hired servants.'"*

*20 "And he arose and came to his father. But when he was still a great way off, his father saw him and had compassion, and ran and fell on his neck and kissed him. 21 And the son said to him, **'Father,** I have sinned against heaven and in your sight, **and am no longer worthy to be called your son.'** 22 "But the father said to his servants, 'Bring out the best robe and put it on him, and put a ring on his hand and sandals on his feet. 23 And bring the fatted calf here and kill it, and let us eat and be merry; 24 for this <u>my son was dead and is alive again; he was lost and is found</u>.' And they began to be merry.*

25 "Now his older son was in the field. And as he came and drew near to the house, he heard music and dancing. 26 So he called one of the servants and asked what these things meant. 27 And he said to him, 'Your brother has come, and because he has received him safe and sound, your father has killed the fatted calf.' 28 "But he was angry and would not go in. Therefore his father came out and pleaded with him.

29 So he answered and said to his father, 'Lo, these many years I have been serving you; I never transgressed your commandment at any time; and yet you never gave me a young goat, that I might make merry with my friends. 30 But as soon as this son of yours came, who has devoured your livelihood with harlots, you killed the fatted calf for him.' 31 "And he said to him, 'Son, you are always with me, and all that I have is yours. 32 It was right that we should make merry and be glad, for your brother was dead and is alive again, and was lost and is found.'" NKJV

This great passage has led countless numbers of people to salvation, but I want you to note a very important point made by the father and how this passage gives us better understanding of the difference between relationship and fellowship.

The son made the decision to break **fellowship** with his father. However, the father never broke the **relationship** with his son, for he did not cease to call him his son, nor did the son cease to call his father, father.

The son made a decision to take his inheritance and squander it with a life of sin, and by his decision, he suffered great loss. He also suffered broken fellowship with his father and brother. There is always a price to be paid for sin. We often think of grace as being free, but the truth that we should never forget is that grace did not come for free. A great price was paid for our sin, our separation from God. Jesus, our **ga'al (Redeemer),** paid the price for our sin and established us **in relationship** with our Heavenly Father God.

There is only one way to leave a **relationship (kinship)**, and that is to willfully give it up as we discover in Heb 6:4-6:

> *For it is impossible for those who were **once enlightened, and have tasted the heavenly gift, and have become partakers of the Holy Spirit**, 5 **and have tasted the good word of God** and the powers of the age to come, **6 if they fall away**, to renew them again to repentance, **since they crucify again** for themselves the Son of God, and put Him to an open shame.* NKJV

Having discovered the difference between relationship and fellowship, we want to examine further the importance of fellowship with God in the Christian's life. First, let us remember that *fellowship* is established around the idea of a common cause, interest, or goal between the people in fellowship.

The first point to be made here is that you and God have a common interest and goal. **Some may ask: What common interest and goal? The answer is simple – you!**

There are many Christians that do not believe God has good things planned for them. However, Jesus tells us in Matt 7:7-12 God's plan for us:

*"Ask, and it will be given to you; seek, and you will find; knock, and it will be opened to you. 8 **For everyone who asks receives**, and he who seeks finds, and to him who knocks it will be opened. 9 Or what man is there among you who, if his son asks for bread, will give him a stone? 10 Or if he asks for a fish, will he give him a serpent?*

*11 If you then, being evil, know how to give good gifts to your children, **how much more will your Father who is in heaven give good things to those who ask Him!** 12 Therefore, whatever you want men to do to you, do also to them, for this is the Law and the Prophets* (God's Law: The law of Sowing and Reaping.)

Jesus was not the first one to reveal the truth (that God has good things for his people); Moses also came to understand it through his fellowship with the Lord. We read about it in Num 10:29-32:

*Now Moses said to Hobab the son of Reuel the Midianite, Moses' father-in-law, "We are setting out for the place of which the Lord said, 'I will give it to you.' Come with us, and we will treat you well; **for the Lord has promised good things to Israel.**" 30 And he said to him, "I will not go, but I will depart to my own land and to my relatives."*

*31 So Moses said, "Please do not leave, inasmuch as you know how we are to camp in the wilderness, and you can be our eyes. 32 And it shall be, if you go with us — indeed **it shall be — that whatever good the Lord will do to us, the same we will do to you."***

Why do so many Christians not understand that God has **good things** for them? It is simply because they have no **fellowship** with God. You cannot know someone, unless you make an effort to know that someone. You may know about them from secondhand sources that you have read or heard, but you only get to know them personally through communication (communion) with them directly. God understands this issue more than we do, and has made it possible for us to know Him through Rhema and Logos. God wants fellowship, **koinonia** (koy-nohn-ee'-ah) with us. It is only through **koinonia** (fellowship, communion, and communication) that we will come to **ginosko** (know fully), God and His ways...the way Abraham, Moses, David, and all the Disciples knew Him.

> *So he cut two tablets of stone like the first ones. Then Moses rose early in the morning and went up Mount Sinai, as the Lord had commanded him; and he took in his hand the two tablets of stone.*
>
> *5 **Now the Lord descended in the cloud and stood with him there, and proclaimed the name of the Lord. 6 And the Lord passed before him and proclaimed, "The Lord, the Lord God, merciful and gracious, longsuffering, and abounding in goodness and truth, 7 keeping mercy for thousands, forgiving iniquity and transgression and sin,** by no means clearing the guilty, visiting the iniquity of the fathers upon the children and the children's children to the third and the fourth generation." Ex 34:4-7*

That which was from the beginning, which we have heard, which we have seen with our eyes, which we have looked upon, and our hands have handled, concerning **the Word (Logos) of life** — *2 the life was manifested, and we have seen, and bear witness, and declare to you that eternal life which was with the Father and was manifested to us* — *3 that which we have seen and heard we declare to you,* **that you also may have fellowship (koinonia) with us; and truly our fellowship (koinonia) is with the Father and with His Son Jesus Christ.**

4 **And these things we write to you that your joy may be full.** *5 This is the message which we have heard from Him and declare to you, that God is light and in Him is no darkness at all. 6 If we say that we have* **fellowship (koinonia)** *with Him, and walk in darkness, we lie and do not practice the truth. 7 But if we walk in the light as He is in the light, we have* **fellowship (koinonia)** *with one another, and the blood of Jesus Christ His Son cleanses us from all sin.*

8 If we say that we have no sin, we deceive ourselves, and the truth is not in us. 9 If we confess our sins, He is faithful and just to forgive us our sins and to cleanse us from all unrighteousness. 10 If we say that we have not sinned, we make Him a liar, and His **word (Logos)** *is not in us.*

How important is *koinonia* for the believer? The more *koinonia* we have with the Holy Spirit, the more we will come to know God, hear His voice, and His plan for our life.

The Rhema and Logos we obtain through *Koinonia* will fill our cup to overflowing, and bring us to the fullness of life and all the good things God has for us. I believe it is this truth that leads Paul to proclaim his amazing prayer for God's people in Eph 1:15-21:

> *Therefore I also, after I heard of your faith in the Lord Jesus and your love for all the saints, 16 do not cease to give thanks for you, making mention of you in my prayers: 17 **that the God of our Lord Jesus Christ, the Father of glory, may give to you the spirit of wisdom and revelation in the knowledge of Him, 18 the eyes of your understanding being enlightened; that you may know what is the hope of His calling, what are the riches of the glory of His inheritance in the saints, 19** and what is the exceeding greatness of His power toward us who believe, according to the working of His mighty power 20 which He worked in Christ when He raised Him from the dead and seated Him at His right hand in the heavenly places, 21 far above all principality and power and might and dominion, and every name that is named, not only in this age but also in that which is to come.*

It is also my prayer that all believers come to the full revelation of the *koinonia* God desires to have with His children. It is then that their spiritual ears will hear the Rhema of God for their life.

Lastly, I close with this thought: Why is it that so many in the Church have such a difficult time accepting that someone can hear the voice of God? As we have examined through history, and the New Covenant, it is God's desire to have *koinonia* with His children. Could it be that those that do not have ears to hear cannot accept the thought that God still talks to His Church today. Or could it be that the enemy has deceived so many into believing no one hears the voice of God? This line of thought is contrary to what Scripture tells us.

1 Thess 2:10-12

> *You are witnesses, and God also, how devoutly and justly and blamelessly we behaved ourselves among you who believe; 11 as you know how we exhorted, and comforted, and charged every one of you, as a father does his own children, 12 that you would walk worthy of* **God who calls you into His own kingdom and glory.**

The word, *calls,* is translated from the Greek word, *kaleo (kal-eh'-o),* which means; to "call" (properly, aloud; to bid; hail or utter in a loud voice (Strong's and Thayer's). In truth, everyone that enters into God's family hears the voice of the Holy Spirit calling them.

The First Call.

What is God saying to you? The first time you hear His voice will be when He calls you into His family. Many have heard His voice call them before, but just ignored or reasoned away His calling. Many are hearing His voice right now. How are you to reply? It is simple! The Apostle Paul describes it best in Rom 10:9-11:

> *If you* **confess with your mouth** *Jesus as Lord, and* **believe in your heart** *that God raised Him from the dead, you will be saved; 10 for with the heart a person believes, resulting*

in righteousness, and with the mouth he confesses, resulting in salvation. NASU

God calls, but it is our responsibility to accept what He is offering. He is offering the completed, redemptive works of the cross by Jesus Christ as payment for your sin. Listen with the spiritual ears of your heart. Accept what God is offering. You will not be disappointed.

Enjoy other books by Dr. Rod Hoskins available at fine bookstores or at the website www.rodhoskinsministries.org.

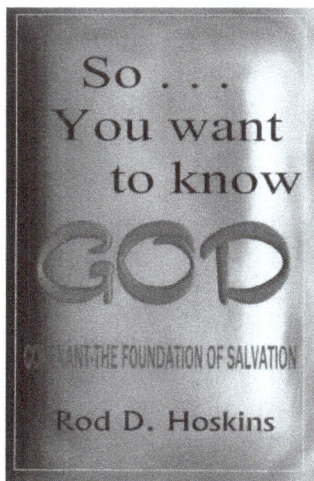

So . . .
You want
to know
GOD

COVENANT-THE FOUNDATION OF SALVATION

Rod D. Hoskins

Over the years, many people have asked about the keys to my success in business. How did a small farm boy start a business from nothing and become a prosperous successful businessman. I tell them it started the day I received the understanding of how God's covenant works. It opened my eyes to the knowledge of how to live in God's Kingdom *today,* and how it is available to every individual that desires to enter into a relationship with Him.

The truth is, people's lives are being destroyed for the lack of knowledge of what they have available to them through God's Covenant. Do you think this is your lot in life and living in *this life victoriously i*s out of reach for you? Discover the answers to many of life's questions in this book. I have been blessed to teach this message around the world and have witnessed life-changing results in God's people.

Destined to Become –

More Than Conquerors

By Dr. Rod Hoskins

Have you ever pondered within yourself: Why is life so hard? How did I get where I am today? Why do I do some of the things I do? Why do I feel like a failure? Can I ever be more than what I am today? Discover new insights about yourself. How God wants to give you victory over strongholds that have hindered you from becoming all that you can be, your entire life. The first step to victory is to learn just what you are fighting against in this life…the who or what that is trying to destroy your ordained destiny? *How do you obtain the Victory?* ***This book will challenge many of your pre-conceived beliefs about yourself and show you how to become More Than a Conqueror.***

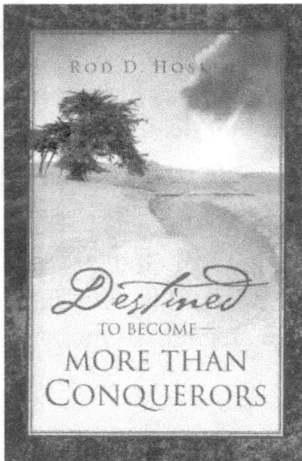

Visit us at www.rodhoskinsministries.org for more Bible teaching on CD and DVD.

or

View us on YouTube at Rod Hoskins Ministries/ Champion Builders Network.

and

Follow us on Facebook at Rod Hoskins Ministries.

www.ingramcontent.com/pod-product-compliance
Lightning Source LLC
LaVergne TN
LVHW051240080426
835513LV00016B/1689